God, Adam, and You

God, Adam, and You

Biblical Creation Defended and Applied

EDITED BY

RICHARD D. PHILLIPS

P U B L I S H I N G
P.O. BOX 817 • PHILLIPSBURG • NEW JERSEY 08865-0817

Unless otherwise indicated, Scripture quotations are from the ESV® Bible (The Holy Bible, English Standard Version®), copyright © 2001 by Crossway, a publishing ministry of Good News Publishers. Used by permission. All rights reserved.

Scripture quotations in chapters 2 and 8 are from the King James Version.

Italics within Scripture quotations indicate emphasis added.

Chapter 10, "Original Sin and Modern Theology," is taken from *Adam, the Fall, and Original Sin,* edited by Hans Madueme and Michael Reeves, published by Baker Academic, a division of Baker Publishing Group, copyright © 2014. It was originally titled "Recent Scholarship on the Doctrine of Original Sin." Used by permission.

ISBN: 978-1-62995-066-2 (pbk.)
ISBN: 978-1-62995-067-9 (ePub)
ISBN: 978-1-62995-068-6 (MobI)

Printed in the United States of America

Library of Congress Cataloging-in-Publication Data

God, Adam, and you : biblical creation defended and applied / edited by Richard D. Phillips. -- 1st ed.
    pages cm
 Includes bibliographical references.
 ISBN 978-1-62995-066-2 (pbk.)
1. Creationism. 2. Creation--Biblical teaching. 3. Bible. Genesis, I-III--Criticism, interpretation, etc. 4. Bible--Evidences, authority, etc. I. Phillips, Richard D. (Richard Davis), 1960- editor.
 BS651.G64 2015
 231.7'65--dc23
                              2014046829

To Dr. C. Stuart Patterson,

gracious servant of Christ and
champion of the doctrine of creation

Contents

Editor's Preface

WHAT DIFFERENCE does Adam make? The answer to some influential Christians today is "not much." Adam, we are told, is a disposable person from biblical lore, who can be safely abandoned to meet the demands of an unaccepting secular culture. Historic Christianity answers differently, however. Adam makes a world of difference when it comes to our understanding of God, mankind, the Bible, and, yes, the gospel. Together with Christians of prior generations, we affirm both the necessity and the importance of the historical, biblical Adam to our Christian faith and witness.

Even if we affirm a historical Adam, however, do we know what he means to the Christian faith today? What does the Bible really say about Adam, and what role does this teaching have in a Christian worldview? Why does Adam matter to our world, and what difference does he make to me? Most significantly, why is God's beginning in Adam inseparable from God's completion in Jesus Christ? These are questions that the contributors answer in *God, Adam, and You*.

Our belief in the Bible's account of the beginning—and especially its teaching on Adam—is important because this issue shapes so many topics of significance. Adam is highly relevant to the question of whether the Bible can be relied upon to tell us the truth about the world's history, even in the face of secular scorn. Adam matters greatly to the way we think about the human race and culture. What does it mean for man to bear the image of God as a distinctive, special creation for the glory of God? What the Bible says about Adam informs us about God, Adam's maker, and the kind of relationship that God desires with us. Most significantly of all, Adam matters greatly to both the great problem of history and its solution in the person and work of Jesus Christ. If the Bible's teaching about Adam is not true, then what of its teaching about Christ? The Bible's beginning, starting with God and Adam, cannot be separated from its end, with its teaching on the believer and Jesus Christ. Given these important issues, it is vital for Christians and churches to defend the Bible's teaching on Adam. More than this, it is essential for us to understand and glory in the vital relationship between creation and salvation as they center on the second Adam, Jesus Christ.

Having the honor of editing this volume, I pray for God to bless these studies for the building up of the reader's faith in Christ and for the extension of God's glory in the world. God told Adam and Eve to "be fruitful and multiply" (Gen. 1:28), a task that the apostle Paul ascribes to the spreading of God's Word during this age of grace (Col. 1:10). May these humble studies spread the knowledge of the Lord on the earth and help Christians to understand their task as followers of the second Adam, the Lord Jesus Christ.

The studies contained in this book arise from the 2013 Philadelphia Conference on Reformed Theology, sponsored by the Alliance of Confessing Evangelicals. In addition to thanking the contributors, I wish to thank Mr. Robert Brady, executive director of the Alliance, together with his outstanding staff. I further wish to thank the host churches for this conference: Byron Center First Christian Reformed Church in Byron Center, Michigan, and Tenth Presbyterian Church in Philadelphia, Pennsylvania.

I am grateful to my dear wife, Sharon, for her tireless support of my ministry and to the session and congregation of Second Presbyterian Church in Greenville, South Carolina, where I am privileged to serve as senior minister. This volume is dedicated to Dr. Stuart Patterson, who for more than a generation has been a stalwart defender of the doctrine of creation in the church, with praise to God and to our Lord and Savior, Jesus Christ.

Richard D. Phillips
August 2014

1

The Bible's First Word

DEREK W. H. THOMAS

In the beginning, God created the
heavens and the earth. (Genesis 1:1)

I REMEMBER IT WELL, for I was a teenager in 1968.
I remember the Christmas message that came from Apollo 8
with a glimpse of planet Earth, which has now become very
familiar to us, but then was something rather new. We all felt a
little smaller as we viewed the earth from an entirely different
perspective. And from somewhere out in space, these words
of Genesis 1 were heard: "In the beginning, God created the
heavens and the earth."

It is no accident, of course, that the Bible begins with God.
God is what the Bible is all about. One of the first lessons that we
learn when reading the Bible is the importance of asking the right
questions. Today people are prone to ask, "What is this passage

saying to me?" We put ourselves in the center hermeneutically. Instead, the first question that we should always ask about any passage of the Bible is, "What is this passage teaching me about God?" For God is first, and he is the center, and he is last.

What Was in the Beginning?

One of the great philosopher-theologians—great, that is, in terms of his influence, rather than in terms of his orthodoxy— Gottfried Leibniz, began his systematic theology with one of the greatest questions that we can ever ask: "Why is there something and not nothing?" Various answers are given to explain why the universe exists. Prominent today is the Big Bang theory, which is so simple, erudite, and perfectly understandable. In the beginning, there was an explosion, and you can visualize it! You can imagine the particles moving out into space. The problem with the Big Bang, however, is that it fails to answer a fundamental question: what was there before the Big Bang? Now, scientists tell us this is an unfair question, but I want to know what is unfair about it. What caused the explosion? For an explosion to take place, there has to be something. Explosions just do not happen in a vacuum. They happen because of a chemical, electromagnetic reaction of some kind. So what was there before the Big Bang?

The Scriptures start, "In the beginning, God . . ." In the beginning was the Lord. In the beginning were the Father and the Son and the Spirit, three persons, one God. There is no express mention here that in the beginning, apart from God, there was nothing. Genesis 1:1 doesn't actually say that God created out of nothing. But, of course, the very absence of any expression, the very absence of any reference to any material, is in itself suggestive of what Moses wants to tell you. The cause of everything that is, he says, is the creative, powerful, and sovereign hand of almighty God.

The first creation story actually ends in verse 3 of chapter 2, where we read, "So God blessed the seventh day and made it holy, because on it God rested from all his work that he had done in creation." In this account, there are references to God's act of creation at both the beginning and the end. They are like two bookends of this first creation story. It is as though God is at the beginning of this story looking forward to what he is going to make, and then at the end of the story he's looking back on what he has made. As we think about the doctrine of creation and the importance of it, I want us to see a number of truths that emerge from this opening prologue, this opening statement of Moses.

Creation Exalts God

First, we should notice a very simple thing: that the biblical doctrine of creation exalts God. We live in a culture, and even in a church culture, where God seems to be without weight. The "weightlessness of God" is what David Wells calls it.[1] One of the great words in the Old Testament for the glory of God is actually a word that is suggestive of weight, much in the sense that some people use the word *heavy* today. If something is significant, they say, "Heavy, heavy." That is, it has weight and depth. God is weighty. God is significant. He is the almighty and sovereign Creator. He is the glorious God who is. Everything that is, the totality of existence—space and time, the vastness of the cosmos,

1. David F. Wells, *God in the Wasteland* (Grand Rapids: Eerdmans, 1994), chapter 5.

everything from the microcosm to the macrocosm—was made to exalt God.

You may enjoy looking at the stars in the night sky. I have an app on my iPad that, when it is tilted up to the sky, identifies the star you are looking at and provides information about it. I was looking at a star recently, as I was walking the dog, and pushed a little button, and it said that the light from this star had begun somewhere in the middle of the sixteenth century. It had taken all those years for it to get here. As a Reformed preacher, I of course mused that the light I was seeing began its journey when Calvin was preaching in Geneva. Extraordinary! The vastness of creation! That light was traveling at 186,000 miles per second from just one of the stars that we can see with the naked eye—not to mention what the Hubble Space Telescope has now given us glimpses of. And all of the universe, in all its vastness, was brought into existence by almighty God. God spoke and there it was. "In the beginning, God created the heavens and the earth."

Instead of looking up at the stars, many scientists are looking down through microscopes into the microcosm of the universe. They are gazing upon the various particles that make up the universe, looking for what they refer to as "the God particle." This is supposed to be a little particle that explains everything. Out of this little particle everything comes, they think. They think that Haydn's *Creation*, Hubert Perry's *I Was Glad*, and everything else comes from this little God particle. As Christians, we mock this idea for the nonsense and silliness that it is. Moses, too, is mocking the idea that something in creation can account for everything, as he begins the Bible with the creation account.

Moses was writing during the exodus to the oppressed Jews emerging from bondage and slavery in Egypt. The Egyptians worshiped the sun and moon and stars, their plethora of gods.

Against this pantheon of gods, Moses writes of Yahweh, the LORD, the sovereign God omnipotent, the only God there is. He made the sun. He made the moon that you bow down to and worship. God made it. He brought everything that is into being. Hebrews 11:3 says, "By faith we understand that the universe was created by the word of God, so that what is seen was not made out of things that are visible." Peter wrote, "The heavens existed long ago, and the earth was formed out of water and through water by the word of God" (2 Peter 3:5). Psalm 33:6 says, "By the word of the LORD the heavens were made, and by the breath of his mouth all their host." Matter, time, and space—everything was brought into being by this sovereign, omnipotent God.

Creation is a work of the Trinity, which is why Genesis 1:2 includes a reference to the Spirit and his role in creation. People ask, "Is the Holy Spirit in the Old Testament?" "What does the Holy Spirit do?" "Does the Holy Spirit come only at Pentecost?" An answer is found in Genesis, chapter 1: "And the Spirit of God was hovering over the face of the waters" (Gen. 1:2). Creation is a Trinitarian act. It is an act of the Father, the Son, and the Holy Spirit. The early church had a little formula for this: *opera ad extra trinitatis indivisa sunt*. This says that "the external operations of the Trinity cannot be divided." All the external acts of God are acts of all three persons of the Trinity. Who created the universe? Who brought it into being? The Father did, and the Son did, and the Spirit did. All three persons of the one God were operative in the work of creation.

Moses' record of creation thus exalts God. One way to see this is in the verb used for *creation*. There are actually three verbs used in the Genesis accounts for *creation*, but a particular word is used in Genesis 1:1: "In the beginning, God *created*" (Hebrew, *bara*). This is a distinctive word because only God is ever its subject in the Bible. Man is never the subject of this verb. God created because he created it out of nothing. It was an act of sovereignty. It was an act of God's particular action. And the very sparing use of this word for creation only magnifies the dignity with which God created the universe.

Genesis 1:1 is saying that matter is not eternal. The Big Bang theory suggests that the universe came into being through a singularity—not technically an explosion, to be sure, but a singularity and an expansion about 13.7 billion years ago. But the question remains, "What was there before the singularity?" If that is how the universe came into being, what was there before the singularity? What caused the singularity? That is not an unfair question, as the secular scientists object. There are a limited number of answers, so let's take them on.

One option is that there was *nothing* before the singularity. Consider this example. If you enter a church sanctuary at midnight, you might say that nothing is there. The people have gone, but in fact many things remain there. The pulpit is still going to be there, the pews are still going to be there, and the organ is still going to be up in the loft. There may be nobody in the building, but that is not nothing. You may go into an empty room, but it is not nothing. Actually there are all sorts of little bits of you floating in the air. It's called dust, and you are shedding it all the time. If a shaft of light comes into the room, you will suddenly see that what you thought was nothing is full of particles. Bearing this example in mind, one explanation of what was there before the Big Bang is that there really was nothing—absolutely nothing at all. And this theory postulates that out of nothing, everything came. And people who believe this cannot accept the resurrection! They find the story of Lazarus coming to life after being dead for three days impossible to believe. It is contrary to medical science, they say. But the whole universe in all of its beauty and complexity supposedly came out of nothing. It makes absolutely no sense whatsoever. It is utterly and completely irrational.

So let's consider another answer. What was there before the singularity and the Big Bang? Perhaps it was ether, hydrogen, or carbon dioxide. Or perhaps there was electromagnetism, and out of it everything came into being. This is scientifically absurd. It is irrational. It is contrary to everything that we know about the universe.

Now, we all trust science to some degree. However much Christians may scoff at secular scientists, we all trust science. I would not get into an airplane as frequently as I do, knowing it will career down the runway at about 150 miles per hour with three hundred people on board, if I did not trust science. You get into your car, switch on the engine, and it works. You trust the science. You need surgery, and so you go to the hospital. You trust the science. Science is not irrational. Yet when science meddles in theology and philosophy, it often becomes absurd. It is speaking beyond its own knowledge.

So what was there before the singularity? It was either nothing or something like hydrogen or electromagnetism. Neither view makes any sense. The Bible's answer is, "In the beginning, God" was there.

I do not mean to advocate a view of the Big Bang at all. I hold to the traditional view of six twenty-four-hour days of creation. God brought the universe into being, and he is perfectly capable of doing that and making it look very old. I have no problems with that whatever. The fact that light, coming from the furthermost parts of the universe, would take longer to get here than the biblical age of this world would allow for, causes me no problem at all. I have no problem with thinking that God created the universe with light already halfway here. What is the problem with that? Why is that so difficult to believe? The essential point of Genesis 1 is simply to exalt God: "In the beginning, God . . ." Why is there something and not nothing? Because God is. Because he always is. He exists eternally. He is the "I AM WHO I AM" (Ex. 3:14). This opening prologue of Genesis is here to exalt the glory, transcendence, magnificence, power, and sovereignty of almighty God.

The Creator-Creature Distinction

A second thing for us to notice is that the biblical doctrine of creation emphasizes the Creator-creature distinction. The first and greatest lesson that you can learn as a human being is that there is only one God—and that you are not that God. You are not the fourth person of the Trinity! Sin, of course, works to confuse this matter. Sin exalts the self, making us into God. John Calvin thus made the famous statement in Book One of his *Institutes of the Christian Religion* that man's mind is a perpetual "factory of idols."[2] Man's mind is an idol-making machine. In Genesis 1, Moses confronts this tendency in the ancient Near Eastern culture and particularly in the cosmology of Egypt. Later, he gives God's name as Yahweh, a name that sounds in Hebrew like the verb *to be*. "I am that I am." The problem with all the Egyptian gods, he insists, is that they do not exist. Moses says to the ancient Near East that the problem with all of their gods is that they do not exist. They do not have being. They exist only in the minds of their creators. But actually they do not exist, because there is only one God, and no human being

2. John Calvin, *Institutes of the Christian Religion*, vol. 1, ed. John T. McNeill (Philadelphia: The Westminster Press, 1960; repr. Louisville, KY: Westminster John Knox Press, 2006), 108.

or created thing is that God. In this way, Genesis 1 underlines the Creator-creature distinction.

Things like pantheism, materialism, dualism, and eternal matter are all ruled out by the opening sentence of Genesis. There is only one God, and we are not that God. Adam was made out of the dust of the ground. Adam was earthly. He was formed, molded, and shaped in the way that an artist shapes contours. As a musician takes notes and shapes them into various sounds and separations of beats and so on, or as a painter takes paint and paints a picture, so God created Adam out of dust. Adam did not have some kind of eternal existence. He is a creature. He is made by God, whose image he bears.

Nowadays, if you look at the label on something that you bought, it is probably going to say "Made in China." I looked on the back of my smart phone, and in very small print that is what it declared: "Made in China." But when you look into the human genome, what you see is a little label that says "Made by God." Created by God. Out of dust we were made and, in the words of Cranmer's great liturgy, "to dust we shall return."[3] This is a fundamental lesson of godliness. It is fundamental to Christianity. We must learn the distinction between the Creator and that which he has created—Creator and creation. We, along with everything that is, belong to creation, belong to something that he has made. But God always is. He always exists.

The Goodness of Creation

A third point made in the biblical doctrine of creation is the goodness of creation. Creation—that is, matter, the stuff of the

3. Thomas Cranmer, *Book of Common Prayer* (1549; repr., Boston: Little, Brown & Co., 1865), 281.

universe—is essentially good. Throughout history—perhaps in Moses' time, but certainly in the time of Jesus and the apostles—there has been the idea that the spiritual and the good are inherently nonmaterial. This idea continues to flourish today. You find it in Plato, and this is one of the ways in which Plato has influenced the Christian church. The idea is that the body is but the prison house of the soul, while salvation is exclusively for the soul. Salvation is something spiritual, involving release from the bondage and captivity of the human body and physical existence. The soul is released into the ether, to float in the universe as something nonmaterial.

Genesis 1 shows the goodness of matter, starting with God's creation of light in verse 3: "And God said, 'Let there be light,' and there was light. And God saw that the light was good." Then in verse 10 he talks about the land and the seas, and they are assigned their respective spheres: "And God saw that it was good." Then again, verse 12 talks about the vegetation and fruit: "The earth brought forth vegetation, plants yielding seed according to their own kinds, and trees bearing fruit in which is their seed, each according to its kind. And God saw that it was good." Then the great heavenly luminaries appear in verse 18: "And God saw that it was good." We read of the advent of animate life in verse 21 and the proliferation of animals in verse 25: "And God saw that it was good." Finally, God created man, male and female. "And behold, it was very good" (verse 31).

Now two things come to the surface immediately. The first thing is that matter itself is not evil. I often have to address this issue in response to a question that arises from my love of my dog. The question is, "Are there dogs in heaven?" My answer is always the same: "Of course." If you think about it, it is a rather silly question. What sort of new heavens and new earth are you actually looking for, if not a restoration of Eden? I like to say to people, "What do you think it is going to look like?" It is going to look like this world, only without sin—as physical and tangible and malleable and structured and visual and audible as this world is, because there's nothing sinful about the world itself. True, this issue is viewed differently by Lutherans and Calvinists. The Calvinist position is not that this world is going to be obliterated because there is something inherently evil in it, but that this world is going to be restored to its designed, stunning beauty.

I was recently in New Zealand to see my daughter and her children. While there, we went on a little tour of New Zealand. It is a staggeringly beautiful country. You drive along a lake with mountains on either side, and you turn a corner and think, "It can't get more beautiful than this." Then you turn another corner and it takes your breath away—the sheer, stunning beauty of it, the goodness of it.

But notice in Genesis 1 that there is good—and then there is very good. Even God says there are standards of beauty. There are layers of aesthetic beauty. Some things are more beautiful than others. There are pieces of music, and some are more beautiful than others. There are works of art. Some of them are trash, and then some of them are absolutely breathtakingly good. Who is the judge? Who is the ultimate judge of what is beautiful? God is.

The creation account in Genesis suggests that there are biblical standards of beauty and biblical standards of aesthetics. Beauty is not just in the eye of the beholder. It's not just what works for you and what works for me. It's not just a kind of cultural elitism that suggests that some things are more beautiful than other things. God is saying here that there are some things that are beautiful and there are some things that are absolutely breathtakingly, staggeringly beautiful. Along the way, the biblical doctrine of creation teaches the essential goodness of creation.

DEREK W. H. THOMAS

A true study of creation will always point to the goal of both creation and redemption. What is the goal of redemption? The goal of redemption is not contrary to creation, but rather to restore creation. Grace is always restorative, as is constantly emphasized in Calvinistic thinking.

Creation as the Basis for Ethics

A fourth point from Genesis 1 is that the biblical doctrine of creation is the basis for morality and ethics. Notice that in the original creation "the earth was without form and void" (Gen. 1:2). Then "God separated" things in verse 4 and again in verse 7. There are some things that are to be separate, and they are not to be joined together. Even though it is possible for man to join them together, God has separated them. We are on the cusp in genetic engineering of doing something, through cloning, that God has separated. Inherent in our createdness is an inward sense of "ought." The fact that we are created produces in us an obligation. We are created in God's image to reflect his glory back to him, to be his servants, to love him, to praise him, and to live for him according to standards that he has laid down. Inherent in creation are the concepts of God's sovereignty and dominion, together with our dependency. The loss of the idea of creation within our modern society explains the slide into degeneracy and immorality. The two go together. When you forget that you are a creature, when you think that you are God, you can then justify doing as you like. You can make up your own laws. You can make up your own morality. You can declare that which is good to be evil and that which is evil to be good. Whatever we think about the length of days in Genesis, the doctrine of creation is fundamentally important to maintaining the standards of ethics and morality: that which God has said is right and that which God has said is wrong.

Outside the biblical worldview of creation, there is, for instance, no argument against homosexuality. There is no basis, outside of a biblical doctrine of creation, for saying that marriage is to be between one man and one woman. This illustrates why creation is so important to ethics and morality. God created the world a certain way. He has set the pattern. He has established the format. The biblical doctrine of creation provides a sound basis for morality and ethics.

Creation as the Ground of Worship

Finally, and perhaps most important of all, the biblical doctrine of creation is essential as the basis, ground, and motivation for worship. Consider Psalm 104:

> Bless the LORD, O my soul!
>> O LORD my God, you are very great!
> You are clothed with splendor and majesty,
>> covering yourself with light as with a garment,
>> stretching out the heavens like a tent. (Ps. 104:1–2)

> O LORD, how manifold are your works!
>> In wisdom have you made them all;
>> the earth is full of your creatures.
> Here is the sea, great and wide,
>> which teems with creatures innumerable,
>> living things both small and great. (Ps. 104:24–25)

> May the glory of the LORD endure forever;
>> may the LORD rejoice in his works,

who looks on the earth and it trembles,
who touches the mountains and they smoke!
I will sing to the LORD as long as I live;
I will sing praise to my God while I have being.
May my meditation be pleasing to him,
for I rejoice in the LORD. (Ps. 104:31–34)

The psalmist is talking about creation. God is the Creator! Knowing God as the Creator inculcates within him a desire to worship, praise, and give glory to God.

We were made for worship. We were made to worship God. Yet outside of union with Christ, we are dysfunctional. We do not know what we are here for. The angst that we find so much in society and in so many of our youth and various forms of culture is but an expression of the loss of identity that we have as God's created beings. God made us for worship. He made us to bring him glory. When we are brought back to him in the gospel, we bow down before him, acknowledging him to be the true and living God, the Creator of the heavens and the earth, who re-creates us in Christ and has promised us a new heavens and a new earth in which righteousness will dwell. When we study creation, it is important to examine the details, as subsequent chapters will do. But it is fundamentally important that we grasp the basic truth that God is the Creator and we are his creatures, remade in Christ to worship him in all of his beauty and glory.

2

The Case for Adam

JOEL R. BEEKE

CARL TRUEMAN has written that the historicity of Adam is the biggest doctrinal issue facing this generation.[1] However, Adam has long had his skeptics. Martin Luther commented, "If Aristotle [the great philosopher] heard this," referring to the creation of Adam, "he would burst into laughter and conclude that although this is not an unlovely yarn, it is nevertheless a most absurd one." Luther said that the mind of fallen men "shows in this way that it knows practically nothing about God, who merely by a thought" made the first man out of a "clod" of earth.[2]

Sometimes people will attempt to graft the word *Adam* onto a concept that is quite foreign to the Scriptures.[3] When I speak of

1. Carl Trueman, "Adam and Eve and Pinch Me," *Reformation 21*, January 14, 2013. Accessed online at http://www.reformation21.org/blog/2013/01/adam-and -evolution-less-import.php.
2. Martin Luther, *Lectures on Genesis*, in *Luther's Works*, ed. Jaroslav Pelikan (St. Louis: Concordia Publishing House, 1958), 1:84. I am indebted to William VanDoodewaard for this reference, and to Paul Smalley for his assistance on this chapter.
3. For example, evolutionists speak of "Y-chromosome Adam" and "Mitochon- drial Eve," but these genetic constructs are totally different from the biblical con- ceptions of Adam and Eve. This evolutionary "Adam" and "Eve" did not even live

Adam, I am talking about a real, historical human being whom God created by a supernatural act to be the father of the entire human race. So when I say that I am making a case for Adam, I am presenting an argument that this man actually lived and did what Genesis 2 and 3 say that he did. Although the wise men and the disputers of this age may laugh at this idea, I am convinced that God has revealed it in his Word, and so I believe it.

A number of people profess to be Christians and yet believe that the human race descended from "a group of several thousand individuals who lived about 150,000 years ago,"[4] and that the first cohort of early humans had evolved from other primates similar to apes.[5] In this view, Genesis 2 is not a literal account of the creation of Adam and Eve, but "a symbolic allegory of the entrance of the human soul into a previously soulless animal kingdom," as one author said.[6]

Pressures for Denying Adam

What are the pressures moving some professing Christians to deny the existence of the historical Adam? One is the theory of macroevolution. Some theologians claim that science "has shown beyond any reasonable scientific doubt that humans and primates share common ancestry."[7] Some scholars have declared that the

---

together in the same era, nor were they the only humans alive at the time. Another example would be C. S. Lewis's proposal that "Adam" might have been a group of highly developed hominids to whom God gave moral and spiritual consciousness (C. S. Lewis, *The Problem of Pain* [New York: Macmillan, 1948], 65, 67).

4. "Were Adam and Eve Historical Figures?," *Biologos*, accessed February 15, 2013, http://biologos.org/questions/evolution-and-the-fall.

5. See R. J. Berry, "Adam or Adamah?," *Science and Christian Belief* 23, no. 1 (2011): 31.

6. Francis S. Collins, *The Language of God: A Scientist Presents Evidence for Belief* (New York: Free Press, 2006), 207.

7. Peter Enns, *The Evolution of Adam: What the Bible Does and Doesn't Say about Human Origins* (Grand Rapids: Brazos Press, 2012), ix.

church must accept evolution.[8] Even some who believe in a historical Adam try to fit him into the theory of the evolution of hominids.[9]

A second pressure comes from the comparison of Genesis to the myths and creation stories of other ancient Near Eastern religions. Since these pagan myths have some similarities to the creation and flood stories, we are told that we must view Genesis as a book that does not claim to tell us historical truth, but only relates religious parables or myths.[10]

In this chapter, I will not make the case against evolution, or that the Old Testament transcends the mythology of ancient cultures. I believe that both cases can be made. Nor will I discuss questions revolving around Genesis 1, the days of creation, and the question of its alleged literary framework.[11] Likewise, I cannot take the time to show through the history of the church that there has been remarkable uniformity of belief in a real Adam, although I highly recommend to you the forthcoming book by William VanDoodewaard, *The Quest for the Historical Adam*.[12]

I will focus upon the testimony of Scripture itself that Adam was a real man. Since I limit myself to "thus saith the Lord,"

8. Such as Peter Enns, Bruce Waltke, Richard Colling, and Tremper Longman III. See Charles Honey, "Adamant on Adam: Resignation of Prominent Scholar Underscores Tension over Evolution," *Christianity Today*, June 2010, 14. These views are actively promoted by the Biologos Foundation (www.biologos.org).

9. Derek Kidner, *Genesis* (Downers Grove, IL: InterVarsity Press, 1967), 28–29; John R. W. Stott, *The Message of Romans* (Downers Grove, IL: InterVarsity, 1994), 164. For similar approaches, see C. John Collins, *Did Adam and Eve Really Exist? Who They Were and Why You Should Care* (Wheaton, IL: Crossway, 2011), 123–31.

10. Enns, *The Evolution of Adam*, chapter 3. Both pressures are noted in Collins, *Did Adam and Eve Really Exist?*, 12.

11. I note in passing that although I do not hold to the framework interpretation, such a view does not necessitate a mythical Adam. See the affirmation of Adam's historicity in Lee Irons with Meredith Kline, "The Framework View," in *The Genesis Debate: Three Views on the Days of Creation*, ed. David G. Hagopian (Mission Viejo, CA: Crux Press, 2001), 220.

12. William VanDoodewaard, *The Quest for the Historical Adam* (Grand Rapids: Reformation Heritage Books, forthcoming).

perhaps someone might consider me to be a theological Neanderthal. But, although science and archaeology are worthy pursuits, if we make them the basis of our faith, we have already stepped off the rock of truth onto the sandy ground of human opinion and speculation. Our faith begins and ends with the Bible. We have received it not as the word of men, but for what it really is: the word of God (1 Thess. 2:13). As the truth of God (John 17:17), it should accomplish its purposes in us as believers (2 Tim. 3:16–17).

I would like to deploy two main lines of argument for the historical Adam, the first from the Bible's history and the second from the Bible's theology. Although we cannot really separate history from theology in the Scriptures, we can discuss the reality of events recorded in Bible history before we draw conclusions as to their spiritual significance.

The Historical Case for Adam

There is good reason to believe that the Bible presents Adam as a real, historical man. I am not claiming that the entire Bible is a historical narrative; the Holy Spirit moved the holy men of God who wrote these books to record his revelation of truth in various genres or literary forms. Just as Jesus Christ was fully God and truly human, so the Bible is truly a human document while its every word expresses God's truth. We recognize that the Bible contains metaphors, poetry, anthropomorphisms, types, allegories, symbolic numbers, parables, and the like. However, we also believe that the Bible contains historical accounts of real people and events.

Let me present four arguments in favor of the conclusion that the Bible portrays Adam as a historical man who lived and acted in time and space.

Argument #1: Genesis Portrays Adam's Creation and Fall as Historical Events

It would do us good if we could set aside all the questions raised by modern science for a moment and just read through Genesis 2–5, letting the Bible speak for itself.[13] Genesis tells us how God made a man from the dust of the ground, placed him in a garden, gave him a law to keep, and then made a woman from the man. It tells us how the Serpent tempted the woman, how the woman and the man disobeyed God's command, how God expelled them from the garden, how they went on to have children, what their children did, and how old the first man was when he died. Later, in Genesis 13:10, we find a reference to the garden of Eden as a geographical location, just as real as the plain of Jordan or the land of Egypt.[14] In other words, Genesis commends the story of Adam to us as history. Even a child can read it and understand this.

In order to overcome the straightforward sense of the text and argue that Genesis 2–4 presents itself as a myth, people raise a number of subtle objections.

Objection #1: By naming him Adam, the generic Hebrew word for "human being," Genesis indicates that he is a symbol for mankind in general or "every-man."[15] On the contrary, while God gave this individual the name for the entire human race because Adam was the father and representative of all humanity, Scripture distinguishes between mankind in general and Adam as a particular human being. Genesis 5:1–3 literally says,

---

13. Genesis 2:4–4:26 is a literary unit in Genesis, marked off by "These are the generations of the heavens and of the earth" (2:4) and "This is the book of the generations of Adam" (5:1). Similar expressions structure the whole book.

14. See also Isa. 51:3; Ezek. 28:13; 31:9, 16, 18; 36:25; Joel 2:3.

15. Berry, "Adam or Adamah?," 31.

This is the book of the generations of man. In the day that
God created man, in the likeness of God made he him; male
and female created he them; and blessed them, and called
their name man, in the day when they were created. And
man lived an hundred and thirty years, and begat a son in
his own likeness, after his image, and called his name Seth.

So sometimes "man" (or *adam* in Hebrew) refers to the whole
race ("and called their name man"), but at other times it refers
to the father of the race ("and man lived an hundred and
thirty years").

Objection #2: Genesis 2 contradicts Genesis 1 by saying
that God created things in a different order, and therefore we
are not to take either account literally. The problem with this
objection is that Genesis 1 and 2 are not contradictory, but
present the same events from complementary perspectives.[16]
Genesis 1 gives us the big picture—the creation of the whole
world, with man created as the pinnacle of God's work. Genesis 2 zooms in on the creation of man, slowing down the
action and focusing our attention upon the garden of Eden.
The two chapters are to be read together in harmony, not set
against each other.

Objection #3: Genesis 3:1 tells us that a "serpent" had a
clever conversation with a woman. Do snakes talk? Obviously
this is a symbolic myth, not a historical account.[17] In answer
to this objection, the Bible indicates that the Serpent was not

16. See Collins, *Did Adam and Eve Exist?*, 52–54.
17. Thus Herman Gunkel's commentary on Genesis, cited in Collins, *Did Adam and Eve Exist?*, 63. A similar objection is that the two trees are magical, and thus this is fantasy. But the two trees named in Paradise are never given magical powers by the text. It is better to see them as sacramental: covenantal signs instituted by God.

just a snake, but a creature possessed and used by an evil spirit. The ancient Israelites would have understood such a connection because in ancient cultures a serpent frequently was regarded as no mere reptile but a spiritual power connected to the idols of this world.[18] This Serpent is no mere snake. Isaiah 27:1 foretells that ultimately "in that day the LORD with his sore and great and strong sword shall punish leviathan the piercing serpent, even leviathan that crooked serpent; and he shall slay the dragon that is in the sea." Revelation 12:9 envisions that same day of the Lord, declaring, "And the great dragon was cast out, that old serpent, called the Devil, and Satan, which deceiveth the whole world: he was cast out into the earth, and his angels were cast out with him."

It is troubling when people claiming to be evangelical or Reformed argue that the Bible contains contradictions or information that we cannot reasonably believe. This sounds too much like the Serpent's question, "Hath God said?" God does say in Genesis 2 through 5 that there was a man named Adam and a woman named Eve, and we should believe his Word. If this part of Scripture is not true and trustworthy, what other parts are not true, and how can we tell which parts are to be believed and which are not?

Argument #2: Biblical Genealogies Present Adam as the Father of Other Historical Persons

Another test for Adam's historicity is how the Bible speaks of him outside of Genesis 2–4. Even if we were not sure of how

---

18. Willem VanGemeren, ed., *New International Dictionary of Old Testament Theology and Exegesis* (Grand Rapids: Zondervan, 1997), 3:85; Geerhardus Vos, *Biblical Theology: Old and New Testaments* (1948; repr., Edinburgh: Banner of Truth, 1974), 34. Thus Rahab, the sea serpent, was an image of the power of Egypt (Ps. 89:10; Isa. 51:9).

those three chapters viewed him, we could find more evidence that Adam was a real man in the genealogies of Scripture.

Our culture does not show much appreciation for genealogies, but other cultures do. Des and Jenny Oatridge were translating the Bible for the Binmarien people of Papua, New Guinea. When they came to a genealogy, the Oatridges thought the people would be bored. Instead, the Binmarien were stunned. They exclaimed, "It's only real people who record their genealogical table. Jesus must be a real person!"[19] We find three genealogies in Scripture that name Adam, and they all testify that he was a real person.

The genealogy in Genesis 5 begins with the creation of Adam and then traces his descendants from Seth to Noah. In each case, it tells us not only who "begat" whom, but also how old the father was when his son was born, and how much longer the father lived after the birth of his son. Clearly this information is presented not as myth or poetry, but as a historical record of the generations of God's people in those times.

There is also a genealogy in 1 Chronicles 1 that begins with Adam and follows his line to Abraham. Richard Pratt writes, "The Chronicler wrote to give his readers a true historical record of Israel's past."[20] If you continue to trace the genealogies through the following chapters, they carry us to David and even through the exile of the kingdom of Judah. The books of Chronicles taught the Israelites to see themselves as the heirs of Adam with respect to both God's curse and his promise.[21]

19. John Hamilton, "No One Bothers to Write Down the Ancestors of Spirit Beings," *John 20:21* (blog), Nov. 2, 2012, http://nornirn.wordpress.com/2012/11/02/no-one-bothers-to-write-down-the-ancestors-of-spirit-beings/. This account appears in Lynette Oates, *Hidden People: How a Remote New Guinea Culture Was Brought Back from the Brink of Extinction* (Brookline, MA: Albatross Books, 1992).

20. Richard L. Pratt Jr., *1 and 2 Chronicles* (Ross-shire, UK: Christian Focus Publications, 1998), 11.

21. Ibid., 64.

Adam's genealogy appears again in the New Testament. Luke 3:23 begins with the Lord Jesus himself and traces his lineage back to David and Abraham, and further back until in verse 38 we read, "which was the son of Enos, which was the son of Seth, which was the son of Adam, which was the son of God."

I am not suggesting that genealogies are empty of theology. It is hugely significant that Luke traces the incarnate Son of God's human lineage back to Adam, who was "the son of God" by creation, as we will see. But we cannot deprive genealogies of their historical character, either. To do this would turn them into nonsense. How seriously would you take me if I showed you my genealogy and it listed Mickey Mouse as my grandfather and Daffy Duck as my uncle? That is just about what we would do to the genealogy of Jesus Christ if we say that Adam was a fictitious character or merely a symbol of humanity in general.

Argument #3: Christ Spoke of Adam, Eve, and Cain as Historical Persons

Our ultimate authority as Christians is the Lord Jesus Christ. We must follow his teachings or we dare not call ourselves his disciples. What do we find when we examine how Christ viewed the history of the Old Testament? John Wenham writes, "He consistently treats the historical narratives as straight-forward records of fact."[22] In presenting his view of the permanence of marriage, Christ specifically cites the words of Genesis regarding Adam and Eve in Mark 10:6–8:

From the beginning of the creation God made them male and female. For this cause shall a man leave his father and

---

22. John Wenham, *Christ and the Bible*, 3rd ed. (Grand Rapids: Baker, 1994), 17.

mother, and cleave to his wife; and they twain shall be one flesh: so then they are no more twain, but one flesh.

Notice what Christ is doing here. In verse 6, he refers to Genesis 1:27, "So God created man in his own image, in the image of God created he him; male and female created he them." Next, in verses 7–8, he refers to Genesis 2:24, "Therefore shall a man leave his father and his mother, and shall cleave unto his wife: and they shall be one flesh." The Lord Jesus ties together the two accounts of man's creation in Genesis 1 and Genesis 2. He treats them as describing the same event—a real event on which we can base our view of marriage today.

Perhaps someone might object that Christ was just making a point about marriage in general. The historicity of Adam and Eve does not matter, they would say, only the theology of marriage. In reply, I would agree that Christ's theology of marriage is very important. We will return to this point. But this does not negate the historical reference. Over all of this teaching, in verse 6, Christ flew this banner: "from the beginning of creation." This is a historical statement about a particular time in history. Right at the beginning of creation, God formed a man and a woman and joined them in marriage as one flesh. Therefore, Christ implied that God created the world and shortly thereafter created a man and gave him a wife. If Christ believed in the historical Adam, why shouldn't we?

We also see that Christ affirms the historicity of the early chapters of Genesis in Luke 11:50–51, where he says,

That the blood of all the prophets, which was shed from the foundation of the world, may be required of this generation; from the blood of Abel unto the blood of Zacharias, which perished between the altar and the temple: verily I say unto you, It shall be required of this generation.

Here again Christ refers to the earliest days of creation: "from the foundation of the world." There, he says, we find the first martyr, Abel, the son of Adam. Christ draws a line from Abel to Zacharias, the son of Jehoiada the priest, who was martyred under the apostate king Joash (2 Chron. 24:20–22).[23] Christ affirms that Abel was just as real as other men recorded in the historical books of the Bible. But the story of Abel in Genesis 4 flows straight out of the story of Adam in Genesis 2 and 3. In fact, Genesis 4:1 begins, "And Adam knew Eve his wife; and she conceived." Clearly Christ treats the accounts of Adam in Genesis as real history. If Christ Jesus, God's Son, our Lord, believed in the historical Adam, then so should we.

These three arguments for Adam bring us to a fourth, which I phrase as a question.

Argument #4: If Adam Was Not a Real Man, Who Else Was Not?

We have seen that Genesis 2–4 speaks of Adam in the context of a historical narrative. Genealogies in the Old and New Testaments list Adam as the historical father of other historical persons. Our Lord Jesus Christ affirms that Adam and his immediate descendants were real persons. As Francis Schaeffer notes, the Bible presents the "concept of creation as a fact of space-time history," on the same level as the other "points of history" that it records.[24]

Let us suppose that after all this, someone still insists that though he believes the Bible to be God's Word, he does

23. In the Hebrew Bible, which is ordered differently from our English Bibles, Genesis is the first book and Chronicles is the last. Thus Christ was drawing a line of martyrdom from the beginning to the end of the Old Testament.
24. Francis A. Schaeffer, *Genesis in Space and Time* (Downers Grove, IL: Inter-Varsity, 1972), 15.

not believe that Adam was a real, historical figure as Genesis describes him.

If that is true, then on what basis should we believe that Abraham was a real person? What about Moses or David? They also appear in historical narratives in the Bible. They are listed in genealogies. They are spoken of as real people by our Lord Jesus. If all that evidence is not enough to prove that Adam was a historical figure, then why should we believe that any of them were historical figures?

If the account of Adam and, by extension, the first chapters of Genesis are not to be taken literally, at what point are we to start accepting the record of the Scriptures as historical? Once we deny the historicity of Adam, we trigger an earthquake that sends a tsunami of skepticism surging over the entire Bible, wiping out its historical reliability. Nor can we build a sea wall that will keep this tidal wave out of the New Testament. I understand that there are some people who deny Adam but still confess Christ. But on what basis? If you reject the reality of Adam, then what reason can you give for believing with certainty that Jesus Christ said and did what the Bible records concerning him? How can you say Adam was a myth, but be sure Christ was real? If you deny Adam's historicity, what is to keep you from denying Christ's physical resurrection?

That is the historical case for Adam. I believe that the historical records of Holy Scripture are sufficient to show that Adam was a real, historical individual. However, there is more we can say. This leads me to my second main line of argument.

The Theological Case for Adam

Adam is not just an interesting figure in history. Adam is foundational in our beliefs as Christians. I suppose that if someone proved that George Washington never existed, it might change the one-dollar bill, but it would not change your life very much. But if Adam disappears into mythology, then we lose the foundation for our views of human identity, human sin, and the Savior of the world. In arguing that the Bible's theology requires a historical, biblical Adam, let me offer six arguments:

Argument #1: The Historical Adam Is the Basis for Believing in Mankind's Original Nobility

If we reject the historicity of Adam, we destroy the basis for the distinction between mankind and the animal kingdom.[25] Genesis 1:26 tells us that God created us in his image and commissioned us to rule over all other earthly forms of animate life. Genesis 2:7 clarifies this further by showing that God did not select or make us out of the existing animals, but created us by means of a supernatural work upon elements taken from the earth. While our bodies share many common characteristics with the animals, the Scriptures insist that man is not just a highly developed animal but a special creation of God, formed as the first man, Adam.

Someone might object that the image of God is not in our bodies, but in our spiritual capacity to know God and our commission from God to rule the earth. Therefore, our bodies could have developed by a natural process of evolution, and "God could have used a miraculous process to create our spiritual

---

25. The evolutionary view of human origins leads logically to a degradation of the value of man. In fact, given the impact of the human race upon other species of plants and animals, some evolutionists and environmentalists believe that it would be best for the world if the human race were largely exterminated. For example, consider the Voluntary Human Extinction Movement (http://www.vhemt.org/) and the purported remarks of Eric Pianka to the Texas Academy of Science in March 2006 (Rick Pearcey, "Dr. 'Doom' Pianka Speaks," *The Pearcey Report*, April 6, 2006, http://www.pearceyreport.com/archives/2006/04/transcript_dr_d.php).

capacities, or used some combination of natural processes and divine revelation to develop these capacities."[26]

In answer to this objection, Genesis 1 does not say that God gave his image to beings that already existed, but that "God created man in his own image" (Gen. 1:27). The image of God is not something added to us, but part of our very constitution. This is so much the case that even after the fall of man into sin and spiritual death, when we are unable to know God in a spiritual way until he makes us alive with Christ, we still retain significant aspects of the image of God, enough for God to make it the basis of his prohibition of murder in Genesis 9:6.

The evolutionary view of the image of God gives us no firm ground for a real distinction between man and animals. In Genesis 9:1–6, the Lord gives man the right to kill and eat animals, but declares that anyone who murders a human being must die because God created man in his image. However, if men are just highly evolved animals endowed (perhaps) with some extra graces from God, then it is hard to understand how we are so different from other animals that we may kill and eat them, but not kill and eat each other. How do we know that God has not given those same graces to other animals? Or how do we know that, as fallen creatures, we have not lost those graces and simply become animals again?

The denial of the historical Adam and the assertion of human evolution blur the difference between mankind and the beasts. On the one hand, this blurring leads us to imputing to animals the rights that belong only to humans, and, on the other hand, it leads us to treat people like so many beasts. Only by believing in the historical Adam are we authorized to confess with David in Psalm 8,

26. "How Could Humans Have Evolved and Still Be Created in the 'Image of God'?," *Biologos*, June 25, 2012, http://biologos.org/questions/image-of-god.

When I consider thy heavens, the work of thy fingers, the
    moon and the stars, which thou hast ordained;
What is man, that thou art mindful of him? and the son of
    man, that thou visitest him?
For thou hast made him a little lower than the angels, and
    hast crowned him with glory and honour.
Thou madest him to have dominion over the works of thy
    hands; thou hast put all things under his feet:
All sheep and oxen, yea, and the beasts of the field;
The fowl of the air, and the fish of the sea, and whatsoever
    passeth through the paths of the seas.
O LORD our Lord, how excellent is thy name in all the earth!

Argument #2: The Historical Adam Is the Root of Mankind's Unity

It is sometimes claimed that Genesis 1–3 is a statement not so much about human history as about Israel's identity, and so "the story of Adam becomes a story for 'every Israelite.'"[27] Thus Adam becomes a mythic figure in a parable analogous to the history of the election and fall of the children of Israel. But Genesis 3:20 says that Adam named his wife Eve because she was "the mother of all living." Genesis, as we saw from the genealogies, presents Adam and Eve as the historical parents of the whole human race.

This leads us to an important theological truth that is lost if we deny the historical Adam, namely, that humanity is one race. Acts 17:26 says that God "hath made of one blood all nations of men for to dwell on all the face of the earth, and hath determined the times before appointed, and the bounds of their habitation." Some translations even say "of one man."[28]

27. Enns, *The Evolution of Adam*, 141–42.
28. In Acts 17:26, Codex Beza (D) and the majority, Byzantine text read *ex henos haimatos* ("of one blood"), a reading supported by the Latin text of Irenaeus and by

Black or white, Chinese or Arab or Russian, we are all blood brothers. We have no basis to view other human beings as fundamentally different from ourselves, for we all share a common set of parents.

Someone might object that our unity is in Christ, not in Adam (Gal. 3:28). But not all men are in Christ, and therefore this cannot be the basis for our view of humanity in general. Furthermore, our unity *in* Christ is based upon our union *with* Christ, and our union with him depends upon his taking of our common human nature to himself in his incarnation as a man. Hebrews 2:11 says that our Savior is not ashamed to call us his brothers because we "are all of one."[29] So even our unity in Christ depends on the fact that our common human nature derives from the historical Adam and Eve.

If we treat Genesis as a collection of myths or metaphors, then we seriously damage our ability to stand against racism. We have opened the door for the idea that various ethnic groups come from different origins. Voltaire, an Enlightenment philosopher who rejected biblical authority, saw Europeans, Africans, and Native Americans as separate species with distinctly different roots.[30] Sadly, some professing Christians have also been guilty of the great sin of promoting racial superiority. We must not let go of the unity of the human race through its one human father, Adam. This conviction is the foundation of true philanthropy, or the love of mankind (Titus 3:4).

Chrysostom, Theodoret, and Bede. The Sinaiticus, Alexandrinus, and Vaticanus uncials (א, A, B), together with some miniscules from the ninth century or later, read *ex henos* ("of one" [masculine/neuter singular]), leading to the translation "of one man."

29. The Greek text of Heb. 2:11 is *ex henos*.

30. Thomas F. Gossett, *Race: The History of an Idea in America*, new ed. (Oxford: Oxford University Press, 1997), 44. This idea that various races come from different origins is known as polygenesis or polygenism. Present mainstream evolutionary theory opposes the polygenesis of man, but it has had advocates in modern times.

Argument #3: The Historical Adam Is the Foundation of Gender Relationships

Our Lord Jesus Christ teaches us to look to the creation of Adam and Eve as the basis for the Creator's order for gender relationships and human sexuality. Matthew 19:3–6 says,

> The Pharisees also came unto him, tempting him, and saying unto him, Is it lawful for a man to put away his wife for every cause? And he answered and said unto them, Have ye not read, that he which made them at the beginning made them male and female, and said, For this cause shall a man leave father and mother, and shall cleave to his wife: and they twain shall be one flesh? Wherefore they are no more twain, but one flesh. What therefore God hath joined together, let not man put asunder.

It is not our purpose here to examine the Lord's teachings about marriage and divorce. But note this: Christ says that we discover God's will for marriage and divorce by looking at Adam and Eve.

The apostle Paul similarly bases his teachings on gender relationships upon the early chapters of Genesis. When explaining how men and women should express male headship in the meetings of the church, Paul writes in 1 Corinthians 11:8–9,

> For the man is not of the woman; but the woman of the man. Neither was the man created for the woman; but the woman for the man.

Again, in 1 Timothy 2:13–14, he says,

> For Adam was first formed, then Eve. And Adam was not deceived, but the woman being deceived was in the transgression.

We must ask ourselves why Christ and the apostle Paul refer to Adam and Eve in their teachings. The answer is found in Christ's words: "he which made them at the beginning." The situation of Adam in Paradise teaches us God's will for mankind precisely because Adam was truly God's first human creation in history. Straight from the Master's hands, pristine and unblemished by sin and the fall, Adam and the manner in which God created him reveal God's will for man. With Adam, God instituted what it means to be a man in relation to a woman.

If we rip the Genesis account out of the flow of history, the Bible loses its authority to reveal God's will for all mankind, for it no longer describes the historical creation of man by God. As a myth, the details about Adam become mere cultural window dressing and not the details of a divinely given, authoritative revelation. But if we continue to view Adam as the first man whom God created, then we are able to apply the Old Testament in the same way that Jesus and Paul did to illuminate what it means to be male and female. In this age, when the church is so ravaged by moral relativism, militant feminism, and homosexual activism, we need a solid basis for our sexual ethics.

Argument #4: The Historical Adam Is the Agent of Mankind's Fall

How do we explain the sin and misery of the human race? Paul writes in Romans 5:12, "Wherefore, as by one man sin entered into the world, and death by sin; and so death passed upon all men, for that all have sinned." Later, in verse 17, he says, "By one man's offence death reigned by one." Paul is elaborating the doctrine of the fall of man, a doctrine attested in Old Testament statements such as Ecclesiastes 7:29: "Lo, this only have I found, that God hath made man upright; but they have sought out many inventions" (see also Job 31:33; Hos. 6:7, marg.).

Paul viewed Adam's fall as a real event in history, and one that determined the shape of all the history that followed. He writes in Romans 5:14 that "death reigned from Adam to Moses." Schaeffer comments, "Adam, it is obvious, is viewed as being just as historic as Moses. If this were not the case, Paul's argument would be meaningless."[31] John Murray says in his commentary on Romans that if we deny "the fall as a literal happening," then it "wrecks Paul's whole argument."[32]

The historical fall of man is pivotal to Christianity. The death of men and women was not God's original design for his "very good" creation. Death came from Adam's historical fall. But if there was no Adam, then we have suffered the agonies and grief of death from our beginning as a race.[33] Denying the historical fall raises a very troubling question about our world. If death and disaster did not arise from the curse and judgment of God upon Adam's sin, then how did it come into God's creation? Did God create a world of evil? Is God perhaps not the all-powerful Creator of all things, but only one limited influence among others? The fall of Adam is the hinge upon which our doctrines of creation and God turn. If we break the hinge, the whole system of biblical doctrine collapses.

---

31. Schaeffer, *Genesis in Space and Time*, 41.

32. John Murray, *The Epistle to the Romans* (Grand Rapids: Eerdmans, 1980), 1:181n18.

33. The Biologos Foundation grossly misuses Calvin's commentary on Genesis 3:19 at this point, claiming that Calvin taught that even if Adam had not sinned, he would have experienced "a more gentle kind of physical death or 'passing' from life into life" ("Did Death Occur before the Fall?," *Biologos*, July 9, 2012, http:// biologos.org/questions/death-before-the-fall). But as these very words of Calvin show, he did not teach that an unfallen Adam would have died, but that he would have been glorified without death.

Furthermore, without Adam's historical fall, we will lose the doctrine of original sin and its accompanying truth that the guilt of Adam's sin is imputed to us, and the pollution of sin is inherited by us, being passed on from mankind's first generation until its last. We will then most likely replace it with the evolutionary idea that mankind is gradually improving.[34] To affirm such a notion, we must reject the doctrinal heritage of the Christian church and embrace theological liberalism. We must reject the teachings of the Bible, which clearly proclaim that all men are under sin's dominion (Rom. 3:9). Paul declares in Romans 5:21 that "sin hath reigned unto death." He explains in Romans 6 that sin is not just a decision or behavior, but an enslaving power from which only the death and resurrection of Christ can free us. Paul clearly believed in the historical fall (see 2 Cor. 11:3; 1 Tim. 2:14).

Although some people try to hold on to the doctrine of sin while rejecting a real Adam and the historical fall, it logically leads into Pelagian theological liberalism and the idea that men will improve if only you put them in a healthy environment. This theological decline into liberalism is what happened to so many Protestant denominations in the late nineteenth and early twentieth centuries. The result is to eviscerate the gospel. Even some who are not evangelicals, strictly speaking, see the weakness of a form of Christianity without the biblical doctrine of sin. In 1937, Richard Niebuhr wrote this description of liberalism: "A God without wrath brought men without sin into a kingdom without judgment through the ministrations of a Christ without a cross."[35]

34. For examples of modern theologians denying the fall, see Collins, *Did Adam and Eve Really Exist?*, 44–47.
35. Richard Niebuhr, *The Kingdom of God in America* (1937; repr., New York: Harper & Row, 1959), 193.

Argument #5: The Historical Adam Is a Type of Mankind's Savior

A "type" is a historical person or institution designed by God to foreshadow Christ and his kingdom in a way that is imperfect, but illuminating. The biblical basis for this language is Romans 5:14: "Nevertheless death reigned from Adam to Moses, even over them that had not sinned after the similitude of Adam's transgression, who is the figure of him that was to come." The word "figure" translates the Greek word *typos* or "type." Paul goes on in Romans 5 to show that whereas condemnation and death fell on those in Adam because of his sin and disobedience, "much more" did justification and life come to those in Christ because of Christ's obedience.

Paul makes the same comparison in 1 Corinthians 15 when discussing Christ's resurrection. He writes in verses 21–22,

> Since by man came death, by man came also the resurrection of the dead. For as in Adam all die, even so in Christ shall all be made alive.

In verse 45, he speaks of "the first man Adam" and "the last Adam." In fact, in verse 47, he speaks of "the first man" and "the second man" as if no one else had ever lived.

There may also be allusions to Adam in Paul's description of Christ as the image of God (Col. 1:15; 2 Cor. 4:4; see also Rom. 8:29; Eph. 4:22–24). Luke also indicates that Christ is like Adam when, as we saw, he traces Christ's genealogy back to Adam, "the son of God," just after Christ was proclaimed "my beloved Son" by the Father's heavenly voice (Luke 3:22–23, 38). It is no mistake that, just after presenting this genealogy, Luke records the temptation of Christ by the Devil in the wilderness, just as Adam was tempted in the garden. But Christ stood against all temptation, whereas Adam fell.

Adam is firmly embedded in the Bible's doctrine of Christ. To see how Christ is the last Adam is the subject of chapter 6 in this book. Our point here is to recognize that Paul is not simply using the history of Adam as an instructive parable or a cautionary tale. He is describing the two great figures in history upon whom everything hangs. If there was no real Adam, then Paul's theology collapses. The apostle would then be profoundly mistaken, not just in his understanding of Adam, but in his doctrine of Christ's work. On the contrary, we believe that Paul was inspired by God, an apostle whose message did not come from man, but was revealed to him by Christ himself (Gal. 1:12).

So far I have argued that not only do the historical records of the Bible make a case for Adam, but the very theology of the Bible makes a case for him. Adam is the basis for mankind's distinctive nobility above the animals, the root of mankind's unity across all ethnic and national boundaries, the agent of mankind's fall into sin and death, and a type of mankind's Savior, Jesus Christ. This brings me to one more theological argument.

Argument #6: The Historical Adam Is a Test Case for Biblical Authority

John Calvin said that the Scriptures are given to us as eyeglasses by which we can properly see and understand God's general revelation of himself and his ways.[36] Without these corrective lenses, our sin-clouded eyes distort what we see in the world. It appears that those who deny Adam have reversed this order. They deny that the Bible says anything authoritative about

---

36. John Calvin, *Institutes of the Christian Religion*, ed. John T. McNeill, trans. Ford Lewis Battles (Philadelphia: Westminster, 1960), 1.6.1, 1.14.1.

scientific matters.[37] On the contrary, they treat modern science as the eyeglasses by which we should read the Scriptures, so that through our scientific knowledge we can sift out God's message from the erroneous beliefs of the ancient community of faith.[38] The result is a view of Scripture that says that God did not breathe his truth into the details of the text, but only inspired its core theological message. Thus they say, "The sacred author was not as concerned about factual details as he was about clearly presenting theological concepts understandable by his intended audience."[39] This is a far cry from the position taken by the Lord Jesus: "The scripture cannot be broken" (John 10:35).

Those who deny the existence of Adam may affirm that "the Bible is the inspired and authoritative word of God."[40] However, they do not mean what evangelical and Reformed Christians have meant by this statement. They do not hold to the Bible's inerrancy, but instead believe that it contains many errors and false teachings derived from the culture and time in which it was written. They also do not affirm the Bible's supreme authority in resolving religious controversies. Instead, the Bible must bow to the changing theories of human science. Ironically, they reject some teachings of the Bible as simply the notions of ancient culture, while they impose other ideas upon the Bible from modern culture. Instead of absolute divine authority governing our faith, we have only the relative authority of human culture and opinion.

37. "Christians today misread Genesis when they try to engage it, *even minimally*, in the scientific arena" (Enns, *The Evolution of Adam*, 33, emphasis added). The Bible is thus shut out of the scientific world.

38. An example of reading Scripture through the lenses of evolution may be found in Richard F. Carlson and Tremper Longman III, *Science, Creation, and the Bible: Reconciling Rival Theories of Origins* (Downers Grove, IL: IVP Academic, 2010), 122.

39. Carlson and Longman, *Science, Creation, and the Bible*, 126.

40. "About the Biologos Foundation," *Biologos*, accessed February 15, 2013, http://biologos.org/about.

For example, Peter Enns readily acknowledges that the apostle Paul believed that Adam was just as real as Jesus Christ. But he says that we need not follow Paul's view, for he was an "ancient man," and we know better today.[41] He also teaches that Paul intentionally twisted the meaning of the Old Testament Scriptures in order to fit his gospel message: "reworking the past to speak to the present."[42] The same man says that the Pentateuch was not written by Moses, but composed piecemeal and brought together after the exile, several centuries after the exodus from Egypt.[43] He corrects conservative evangelicals for believing that if the Bible is God's Word, then it must "be historically accurate in all its details."[44] Instead, God "adopted mythic categories" from the ancient world, myths that we may now discard, so long as we retain the kernel of truth they contain.[45] These are clear and sobering examples of how denying the reality of Adam puts one on a trajectory to deny the full trustworthiness of the Holy Scriptures. It would turn the Bible into a collection of fables, or mythic stories with a spiritual or moral point, as if all Scripture were one long parable and not a mixture of doctrinal instruction, historical narrative, poetry, proverbs, epistles, prophetic oracles, parables, allegories, types, and apocalyptic literature.

Those who take this route perhaps may not realize that they are departing from the path of biblical orthodoxy and following the same road as unbiblical neoorthodoxy. Emil Brunner (1889–1966), a prominent neoorthodox theologian, said that the Bible's teaching on creation is "not a theory of the way in which the world came into existence," but only a summons to

41. Enns, *The Evolution of Adam*, xvi–xvii, 139.

42. Ibid., 113.

43. Ibid., 23.

44. Peter Enns, *Inspiration and Incarnation: Evangelicals and the Problem of the Old Testament* (Grand Rapids: Baker Academic, 2005), 47.

45. Ibid., 53.

know God as your Lord and Creator.[46] Thus, he said, the Adam of Genesis 2 is inseparable from ancient beliefs about the universe and cannot be viewed as a real individual in light of our modern understanding.[47] For Brunner, Paradise was "myth" not "historical fact."[48]

It is not necessary for us to go in this direction. Why couldn't the ancient Hebrews have understood it if God had told them that he created by a long, slow process of evolutionary change? Every day, as they planted and harvested crops or worked with sheep and cattle, they could see change and improvement in the various seeds they planted or the animals they bred. Why couldn't God effectively communicate to them that he had conferred a human soul upon an existing animal rather than breathed life into a body formed directly out of the earth? Why not reveal in Genesis that God made many human beings at first, instead of just one? Why would these things have been harder for them to accept than the idea that there is only one true and living God, given that all their neighbors worshiped many gods? And why must we separate the way in which God created from the fact that he is Creator? Does it not glorify God as Lord to know that he created man, not through any natural process, but by a supernatural act of special creation? Yes, the account of the historical Adam's creation greatly honors God as Creator and Lord.

Furthermore, this is a dangerous direction to go. If the Bible is a mixture of cultural dressing wrapped around divine truth, then how can we be sure which part is the husk and which is the kernel? What one generation embraces as the kernel of

46. Emil Brunner, *Dogmatics*, vol. 2: *The Christian Doctrine of Creation and Redemption*, trans. Olive Wyon (Philadelphia: Westminster Press, 1952), 7–8.

47. Ibid., 50.

48. Ibid., 74. On Brunner and Adam, see Bernard Ramm, *The Christian View of Science and Scripture* (Grand Rapids: Eerdmans, 1954), 318–19.

divine truth could very well be rejected by another generation as merely more human culture and tradition. We see this happening around us even now with respect to the definition of marriage and homosexuality.

Conclusion: History and the Christian Faith

In making a case for the historical Adam, I have employed two main lines of argument. First, I have argued that the history taught by the Bible presents Adam as a man who was just as real as Abraham, Moses, David, and the Lord Jesus Christ. Second, I have argued that the theology taught by the Bible presents the history of Adam as an essential part of our view of God, man, and Christ. By now it should be clear that though I presented these as two distinct lines of argument, biblical theology cannot be separated from its setting in history without doing grave damage to the integrity and trustworthiness of the Holy Scriptures.

One of the great problems involved in the denial of Adam is that it separates the message of the Word of God from the history it records. This separation destroys the credibility of its message. The Bible tells us a grand story that begins with creation and finds completion in a new creation. It is not myth, but gospel.[49] *Gospel* means "good news," a message about events that happened and their happy consequences. Without the events,

49. *Myth* commonly means "fable." The Greek word appears in the NT in the sense of religious fictions (1 Tim. 1:4; 4:7; 2 Tim. 4:4; Titus 1:14; 2 Peter 1:16). It is difficult to define *myth* in the sense that some scholars use it, but even in academic usage it continues to suffer from a sense of a story whose events are not regarded as true. Thus Enns's definition of myth, "an ancient, premodern, prescientific way of addressing questions of ultimate origins and meaning in the form of stories," still smacks of modern arrogance looking back at ancient beliefs with an air of superiority (Enns, *Inspiration and Incarnation*, 40). See Collins, *Did Adam and Eve Really Exist?*, 29–31.

there is no news to tell. As Paul says in 1 Corinthians 15:17, "If Christ be not raised, your faith is vain; ye are yet in your sins." It is no mere coincidence that most of the articles of the Apostles' Creed refer to historical events, not theological concepts. The Christian faith is built on history. In the end, if you undermine its historical foundations, then the whole of Christianity collapses into subjective opinions and feelings. But mere subjective feelings cannot save you.

Biblical history is not like Aesop's fables—charming stories about a fox and a stork or a mouse and a lion that we can apply to ourselves by way of analogy. Rather, the Bible is telling us our history, just as knowing your family history can help you to understand your life today. As one author said, when we read the Bible, "we must understand that we dwell in the same history." C. John Collins says that the Bible gives us "a grand narrative or worldview story," and each of the people of God should see himself as "an heir of this story, with all its glory and shame; as a steward of the story, responsible to pass it on to the next generation; and as a participant, whose faithfulness could play a role, in God's mysterious wisdom, in the story's progress."[50] Adam should be as real to you as your own father, because Adam is your father. As both a human being and a fallen sinner, you are what you are because of what Adam was and what Adam did.

Has this ever become an experiential reality for you, such that you have confessed that if you had been Adam in Paradise, you too would have fallen? Have you ever felt the guilt of Adam's sin imputed to you and the pollution of sin passed on to you? Although space prohibits, an experiential case could also be made for a historical Adam. For the purpose of this chapter, that expe-

---

50. Collins, *Did Adam and Eve Really Exist?*, 40–41. The first quote is from Alan Jacobs, *Shaming the Devil: Essays in Truthtelling* (Grand Rapids: Eerdmans, 2004), 89, cited by Collins.

riential case is not as important as the historical and theological case, but for a Spirit-led believer, the daily experiential warfare of Romans 7:14–25, which leads to the cry, "O wretched man that I am," is a compelling subjective case that underscores the reality of Adam's fall.

We must honestly face what the text of Holy Scripture is claiming, whether or not we like it or can square it with the present views of most scientists. As Bible scholar E. J. Young says, it is far more honest to say, "Genesis purports to be a historical account, but I do not believe that account," than it is to say, "I believe that Genesis is profoundly true," but is a myth or some kind of poetry.[51] That is double-mindedness, not honest interpretation.

Some people sincerely hope to wed evolutionary biology and the Christian faith by denying the reality of Adam. They believe that they are finding a middle ground between naturalistic science and biblical fundamentalism. They may hope that they have opened the door for atheistic scientists to come in and dialogue fruitfully with Christian believers. But they fail to see that in opening such a door they have given away the citadel. The denial of the historical Adam brings with it a host of ideas contrary to the Christian view of creation, human nature, human relationships, and the fall of man. Without this foundation, there is no place to stand for the gospel of redemption by the sovereign grace of God in Jesus Christ. This is not the way to make Christianity palatable to modern ears, but rather is to bring in a Trojan horse by which false doctrine can invade and devastate true Christianity.

We need to remember that the Word of God is always true and our basis of truth. Science is continually changing. Our

51. E. J. Young, *In the Beginning: Genesis 1–3 and the Authority of Scripture* (Edinburgh: Banner of Truth, 1976), 19.

defense of truth is the teaching of the biblical text, not a scientific reconstruction of the text or ideas read between the lines of the text. E. J. Young puts it well:

> Whenever science and the Bible are in conflict, [we are told that] it is always the Bible that, in one manner or another, must give way. We are not told that science must adjust its answers in light of Scripture. Always it is the other way around. Yet, this is really surprising, for the answers which scientists have provided have frequently changed with the passing of time. General revelation is to be interpreted by special revelation, nature by Scripture, "science" by the Bible.[52]

I am not judging those who deny a literal Adam, but I am passing judgment on their doctrine. Could it be that they are still clinging to Christ by faith in some way? We can all live with astonishing contradictions and inconsistencies in our beliefs. But their doctrine launches people on a trajectory that will ultimately lead to apostasy. Remember the famous words of R. D. Wilson, founding Old Testament professor of Westminster Theological Seminary: "Never fear! God's world never contradicts God's Word." We should therefore cling to the faith once delivered to the saints and let no one steal our reward.

The day will come when we will look our father Adam in the face and know the truth of the matter beyond all doubt. And, happily, we believers will also look the second Adam in the face and know the truth of all truth beyond all doubt. *Soli Deo gloria!*

---

52. E. J. Young, *Studies in Genesis One* (Phillipsburg, NJ: Presbyterian & Reformed, 1976), 53–54.

3

Two Views of the Human Person

KEVIN DEYOUNG

MANY OF THE MOST controversial issues, not only in the church but in our culture, can be traced back to differing views of the human person. We have debates today about sexuality, gender, origins, how you counsel someone, eternal punishment, where war comes from, and the nature of government, marriage, and abortion. Any list of the ten most debated hot topics in our culture would all have ties to this question: who are we? Generally speaking, there are two competing views of the human person. Often when issues come to us, they come to us at the end of a long train of argument. So we see the caboose, but do not see everything that comes before. We are just getting the end of the argument. But if we trace most hot-button issues back, we see that at bottom we have two very different views of the human person. What does it really mean to be human?

Growing up, one of the cartoons I watched from time to time was *Scooby Doo*. That show was very formulaic. Every episode ended with somebody pulling off a mask to be revealed. Then you knew who had committed the crime: it was the groundskeeper, and there he was. But then another groundskeeper would walk in, and you would have two. Shaggy would say, "Zoinks," and you would have to figure out what was going on. Finally, one of them would take off the mask, and you would realize who the real person was.

What does it mean to be human? What is under the mask? The world and the Bible have different ways of describing the human person. Only one of them can be right. Here are the two views of the human person that I want to unpack, using five contrasts:

1. According to the world, we are (1) here by chance, (2) free to create our own selves, (3) basically good, (4) ethically excusable, and (5) destined for a happy heaven or a blessed extinction.
2. According to Scripture, we are (1) here by design, (2) created to reflect God's image, (3) fundamentally flawed, (4) morally culpable, and (5) destined to worship God in heaven or face his just wrath in hell.

By Chance or by Design?

First, are we here by chance or by design? The first verse of the Bible gives us the answer to one of the most enduring questions in the history of the world: why is there something rather than nothing? Either the universe is the work of some free, personal agent or it somehow created itself. Genesis 1 answers the question clearly: "In the beginning, God . . ." (Gen. 1:1). God created. We are here by his design. In the Apostles' Creed, we confess that "God the Father Almighty" is the "Maker of heaven and earth." Psalm 8:4–5 says,

> What is man that you are mindful of him,
> and the son of man that you care for him?
>
> Yet you have made him a little lower than the heavenly beings
> and crowned him with glory and honor.

Psalm 139 states that each of us was individually formed, knit together in our mother's womb. That is what the Bible says so clearly: we are here by design.

And yet the world tells a different story. In the beginning was nothing, and then it blew up. From that primordial state, over millions of years, lower life became intelligent life, and human life evolved by random selection over millennia of chance. There are staggering and depressing implications that flow from this evolutionary worldview. George Bernard Shaw wrote several generations ago, "When [evolution's] whole significance dawns on you, your heart sinks into a heap of sand within you. There is a hideous fatalism about it, a ghastly and damnable reduction of beauty and intelligence, of strength and purpose, of honor and aspiration."[1] Or consider H. G. Wells in his fantasy *The New Republic*, where you see some social Darwinism:

> How will the new republic treat the inferior races? How will it deal with the black? . . . the yellow man? . . . the Jew? . . . those swarms of black, and brown, and dirty-white, and yellow people, who do not come into the new needs of efficiency? Well, the world is a world and not a charitable institution, and I take it they will have to go.[2]

---

1. Quoted in Richard Dawkins, *A Devil's Chaplain* (New York: Mariner Books, 2004), 9.
2. Ibid., 10.

Richard Dawkins, one of the new atheists, actually began one of his books with those quotes from George Bernard Shaw and H. G. Wells in order to make the point that he disdains them and disagrees with their thinking. He describes Wells's vision as "blood-chilling" and commits himself to fight against it. Dawkins dislikes the moral implications of the evolutionary worldview that he so fervently propagates. He says, "At the same time that I support Darwinism as a scientist I am a passionate anti-Darwinian when it comes to politics and how we should conduct our human affairs."[3] Dawkins is thus committed to a chance universe driven by natural selection, the implications of which he cannot accept. As he realizes, a creation without a Creator is a scary thought.

Are we here by chance or by design? I am not a scientist, but you can read scientists who give many reasons to believe that even from science itself there is good evidence for a Designer. Even Dawkins says, "Biology is the study of complex things that *appear* to have been designed for a purpose."[4] Yes, they do appear that way. Richard Lewontin, another evolutionary biologist, admits that living organisms "appear to have been carefully and artfully designed."[5] They recognize that there is an appearance of design. Hugh Ross is well known for describing the anthropic principle, which means that all of the scientific variables need to be working in exact alignment—and are—so that planet Earth can support human life. He has a list of dozens of these characteristics: the galaxy size, the galaxy type, the galaxy location, the star location, star mass, star

3. Ibid., 10–11.

4. Richard Dawkins, *The Blind Watchmaker: Why the Evidence of Evolution Reveals a Universe without Design* (New York: Norton, 1996), 1.

5. Richard Lewontin, "Adaptation," *Scientific American* (September 1978), quoted in Paul E. Little, *Know Why You Believe* (Downers Grove, IL: InterVarsity Press, 2008), 38.

color, white dwarf binary types, the tilt of our axis, the force of the tides, the magnetic field, the thickness of the earth's crust, the oceans-to-continent ratio, the oxygen level in the atmosphere, the water vapor level, the tectonic activity, and on and on. All of these are necessary in just the right proportion for human life to exist.[6]

Michael Behe has coined the term "irreducible complexity," arguing that there are certain molecular structures that could not have evolved from simpler structures. He said it is like a mousetrap, which evolutionary gradualism cannot explain, because if you have this structure in a less complex form, it will not function.[7] Then there is Stephen Meyer, who has worked with DNA. He notes that there are four nucleotide bases, known by the letters A, T, C, and G, which are combined in long sequences in DNA. Scientists have discovered that this sequence of gene coding does not consist of repetitive information. Nor does it display mere randomness. Instead, it manifests a specified complexity, as if speaking a language. Meyer argues that there is a design signature written into our cells. The sequence even of these bases says something and produces information for the cell to build proteins and to function.[8]

All this evidence speaks of a design stemming from a common ancestral source, Adam and Eve. Because of this common ancestry, we can insist on universal dignity and justice and understand a common purpose or design. One of the uniquenesses of a Christian worldview is that history has a beginning point and an ending point. It is going somewhere. We are not just random

6. See Hugh Ross, *The Creator and the Cosmos: How the Greatest Scientific Discoveries of the Century Reveal God* (Colorado Springs: NavPress, 1995), chapter 14.

7. See Michael J. Behe, *Darwin's Black Box: The Biochemical Challenge to Evolution* (New York: Free Press, 2006).

8. Stephen C. Meyer, *The Signature in the Cell: DNA and the Evidence for Intelligent Design* (New York: HarperOne, 2010).

bits of chance evolved by the luck of protein strands, but there is indeed a signature in the cell.

So why are we here? By chance or by design? The Bible clearly says we are here by design.

Self-Image or God's Image?

The second issue is this: are we free to create our own selves, or are we created to reflect God's image? The Bible says we are meant to reflect God's image, which theologians look at from a number of different angles. This speaks of *resemblance*—who we are in our intelligence and appreciation for beauty and rationality. We are moral beings with the capacity for worship and for language. The image of God also speaks of *relationship*—how we interact with God and others. When Paul speaks of the image of God being renewed, he says it is being renewed in knowledge and holiness in how we interact with each other (Col. 3:10). There is also a *representational* dynamic to the image of God—how we exercise dominion as rulers, as stewards, as those who mirror in some way Adam's calling to be the lord of the garden and to cultivate it. This is where much of modern environmentalism takes a wrong turn. As Christians, we agree with enjoying the beauty of God's creation and not despoiling it. Yet modern environmentalism often assumes that human beings are intruders into a pristine, natural environment. Human beings are considered constant threats, rather than those who are called to cultivate the world around us. Think of the computer revolution, which is based on little silicon chips made from sand. God has given us ingenuity and creativity so that we can cultivate the resources he has given us to turn them into something useful.

The world says you are free to create who you want to be. You are created not for divine exaltation but for self-exploration. You are made not to be stamped with a divine impression but to spend your life expressing yourself. You just have to watch a few commercials. Cingular sells cell phone service with the slogan "Express yourself." Dr. Pepper has commercials in which everyone is wearing a maroon Dr. Pepper shirt while singing and marching through town, with the motto "Be you." Even the U.S. Army had a recruiting slogan that trumpeted an "Army of one." What is assumed is that you are a blank slate. Whatever you have chosen to paint on the canvas of your life is beautiful because you have painted it. Of course, that worldview works less well in math or in a real job. It is hard to think that it would be a good principle for your whole life.

This project of self-definition goes much broader and deeper than we sometimes think. For many people in the world, self-expression and self-exploration are necessary to make sense of life. That is why, when the Christian message tells people that their self-exploration has God-given limits, they have no ears to hear it. Anna Quindlen, who has written for the *New York Times* and *Newsweek*, had this to say a number of years ago to a group of graduating seniors:

> Each of you is as different as your fingertips. Why should you march to any lockstep? Our love of lockstep is our greatest curse, the source of all that bedevils us. It is the source of homophobia, xenophobia, racism, sexism, terrorism, bigotry of every variety and hue, because it tells us there is one right way to do things, to look, to behave, to feel, when the only right way is to feel your heart hammering inside you and to listen to what its timpani is saying.[9]

9. Quoted in Richard John Neuhaus, "Scandal Time III," *First Things*, August 2002. Accessed online at http://www.firstthings.com/article/2002/08/scandal-time-iii.

Of course you don't have to look very hard to see the internal contradictions in Quindlen's statement. If it is true that there is not one right way of doing these things, why would she condemn homophobia, xenophobia, racism, sexism, terrorism, and bigotry? By what grounds does she put those in the category of bad things to avoid? And what if your drum doesn't beat in time with the God of the universe?

We have been told over and over that there is a god within, and that if we would just look deep enough within, we would find the source of our inspiration. We have been told in a hundred different Disney movies and a thousand TV shows that the purpose of life is to find the real me. Instead of "I desire to know nothing but Christ and him crucified" (see 1 Cor. 2:2), we now say, "I desire to know nothing but the self and it Oprah-fied." We are always told to dig deeper and find new insights—not from God, not from his Word, but from the deeper recesses of our own hearts and brains. What is wrong with you is that you are not in touch with the real you. If you could find the real you that is underneath all the bad stuff about you, then you would be set free. That is the quest, that is what salvation is—to get in touch with who you really are.

I recently read a book about college admissions. It was actually quite a funny book. In it, the author writes about a University of Chicago admissions question that he and his son encountered. I once visited the University of Chicago and thought about going there. I am glad I didn't run into this question:

> Names have a mysterious reality of their own. We may feel an unexpected kinship with someone who shares our name or may feel uneasy at the thought that our name is not as much our own as we imagine. Most of us do not choose our names. They come to us unbidden sometimes with ungainly

sounds and spellings, complicated family histories, allusion to people we never knew. Ruminate on names and naming and your name's relationship to you.[10]

The author reports that the counselor told him, "Your son has to dig deep. He has to talk about his innermost thoughts." The dad writes in the book,

> I shuddered. He's a seventeen-year-old boy! I wanted to tell her: Seventeen-year-old boys do not have innermost thoughts—and if they did, neither you nor I would want to know what they are. And in any case, it's kind of impertinent of an admissions committee to make such a demand. Who are they to force a catharsis on seventeen-year-olds? The kid is just applying to their college, not asking for their hand in marriage.[11]

Many of us have found a wonder, out of everything else in the whole wide world, that can occupy our deepest affections and our highest thoughts for a lifetime, and the name of that wonder is me. Or you. God created us in his image, and since then we have been intent on creating him in our image. For many people, God turns out to be nothing more than the true self that we seek to find buried beneath the rubble of religion and doctrine and unmet expectations. That's the way the world understands the human person.

Writing over a hundred years ago, G. K. Chesterton said in his classic book *Orthodoxy*:

> That Jones shall worship the god within him turns out ulti-mately to mean that Jones shall worship Jones. Let Jones

10. Quoted in Andrew Ferguson, *Crazy U: One Dad's Crash Course in Getting His Kid into College* (New York: Simon & Shuster, 2012), 137.
11. Ibid.

worship the sun or moon, anything rather than the Inner Light; let Jones worship cats or crocodiles, if he can find any in his street, but not the god within. Christianity came into the world firstly in order to assert with violence that a man had not only to look inwards, but to look outwards, to behold with astonishment and enthusiasm a divine company and a divine captain. The only fun of being a Christian was that a man was not left alone with the Inner Light, but definitely recognized an outer light, fair as the sun, clear as the moon, terrible as an army with banners.[12]

Our culture is awash in narcissism. And this is not just being on Facebook and having a blog and doing Twitter (though I am guilty of all three). The problem goes deeper. Jesus says we cannot serve two masters (Matt. 6:24), and our world would have us serve the self. Orthodox Christianity says, "Let me take God, that I might die to myself." And there are many churchgoers in between who would like to choose both. They say, "I want to worship God, so that he might give me the full experience and exploration and triumph of myself." That is what passes for Christianity in too many churches—a gospel-less, worldly way of looking at our design, our purpose, and our dignity. Are we here to reflect God's image, or are we here for our own self-exploration and self-exaltation?

Basically Good or Fundamentally Flawed?

Here's the third contrast. Are we basically good or fundamentally flawed? Of course, the Bible teaches that, since the first Adam, we have come into this world fundamentally flawed. "None

12. Gilbert K. Chesterton, *Orthodoxy* (London: John Lane, 1909), 136–37.

is righteous," says Romans 3:10. "All have sinned and fall short of the glory of God," writes Paul in Romans 3:23. Jeremiah says, "The heart is deceitful above all things, and desperately sick" (Jer. 17:9). The natural man is "dead in . . . trespasses and sins" (Eph. 2:1), having been conceived in sin and brought forth in iniquity (Ps. 51:5). This understanding of the human person was one of the principles on which this country was founded. I realize that some Founding Fathers were evangelical Christians and some were nothing of the sort. But you can read, for example, James Madison in *The Federalist Papers* talking about the need for checks and balances in a system of government, arguing "that the nature of man is not the nature of angels, that we are prone to rivalries and ambitions."[13] The American republic was laid out with an understanding that human avarice, selfish ambition, and the fallenness of our nature must be held in check as best we can.

This has a lot to say about the problems in the world. Do we ask how we can mitigate the fallen tendencies of our nature and nations so that we can minimize the effects of war and the frequency of war as much as possible, humanly speaking? Or do we say that there is war and conflict because people have not received enough education or have not talked to each other kindly enough? There are very different ways in which we approach all sorts of issues in our world based on whether we think people are basically good or have a built-in predilection to sin. The world hates the doctrine of original sin because it frustrates its plans for utopia, because it is a blow to our self-esteem, and because it undermines one of the central fallacies of our day. That fallacy is this: is equals ought. Whatever you are, in this view, is how you ought to be. Whatever your desires are, they are to be let loose—not redirected, transformed, subjugated, or put to death.

13. James Madison, "Federalist No. 51," in *The Federalist Papers*, ed. Charles R. Kesler and Clinton Rossiter (New York: Signet, 1999), 319.

Lady Gaga is a hugely popular singer today, and one of her best-known songs is called "Born This Way." The idea is that we can love ourselves for being who we are—God doesn't make mistakes. She goes on to say that you can be whatever gender you want to be, or have whatever sexuality you want to have, because you are born that way. We can look at that song with easy disdain, especially if we are from a generation that would never listen to Lady Gaga, and yet we are kidding ourselves if we don't think that that is the air that especially younger generations are breathing. There is nothing controversial in that song for large swaths of the American population.

Christians need to have some savvy to approach this sort of assumption and say, "There is a powerful half-truth here. We cannot be other than we are." This is tapping into a Christian understanding at one level, that our identity does determine what sort of life we live. But here is the great mistake: the world assumes that by nature you are who you ought to be, but the gospel tells you that by grace you can be who you ought to be. Is equals ought only when you are joined to Christ, when you have union with him through faith. That is really Paul's ethic in Romans 6. You belong to Christ. You died to sin. You are alive to him. Now go and live this way. That is who you are. You cannot be other than what you are. The message we need to give the world is that God made you a certain way, but sin made you the way that you are now, and God can remake you in his way of grace and eternal life.

Ethically Excusable or Morally Culpable?

Here is a fourth contrast. Are we ethically excusable or morally culpable? The world is constantly finding ways to make us ethically excusable. One way is to say that you are just a product of your own history or environment. The most popular excuse today is biological determinism: you are all hardwired. The result is that there is a label and a gene to explain everything.

People who know me can attest that I have, shall we say, a very refined palette. I grew up in a Dutch home where salad was Jell-O, so I never learned to eat vegetables. The truth is that I do not eat well at all. I was recently at the doctor getting some tests, and he said, "Has your diet changed recently?" And I thought, "Not since I was four: chicken nuggets, hamburgers, hot dogs, French fries, two percent milk."

I was therefore interested when a friend sent me an article that identifies a new disease that has been called SED—Selective Eating Disorder. The article contained stories about people who had a bad experience with a food once or in a dream, and now ate selectively. So now I have a label! I am no longer a picky eater. I have Selective Eating Disorder. My insurance should cover it.

There are of course legitimate problems that people have, some of which involve a mix of spiritual concerns with biological issues. But the situation now is that when we get a label, we automatically shift from the realm of volition and responsibility to the realm of medicine and the unavoidable. We use this language all the time as if we are merely passive recipients, not active agents. The media declares this whenever a horrific crime takes place, like a mass school shooting. The cause for this evil behavior is always located somewhere outside the self. It was because of video games or strange novels, or because the shooter was too right-wing or left-wing, or because he grew up in a culture of hate. Whenever an internal cause is suggested for the perpetrator of the crime, it is always described in such a way that it doesn't really belong to him. It is either a psychological disorder or "personal demons"—some kind of invading force from the outside. We instinctively resort to passive speech, unable to bear the thought that perhaps a wicked person has perpetrated a wicked crime because the human heart is desperately sinful and capable of despicable sin. No one commends the crime, but few are willing to condemn the criminal either. In such a world, we are no longer moral beings with a propensity for righteousness or evil. We are instead the product of our circumstances, our society, our upbringing, and our biochemistry. And the only way we have to talk about our problems is in the language of therapy, disorder, and dysfunction.

The world, to a large extent—and even the church—has lost the ability to speak in moral categories, as befits moral agents made in the image of a moral God. So we have preferences instead of character. We have values instead of virtue. We have no God of holiness and no Satan either. What we have are breakdowns, crack-ups, maladjustments, inner turmoils, and insecurities. We do not speak of the fear of man, the love of praise, and the sin, adultery, treachery, and rebellion of the human heart. We think this loss of language will make the world more palatable, but in fact it makes the world a more dangerous place. For though the words disappear, the reality does not. We may get rid of the language, but the reality is still present.

Destined for Heaven or for a Glorious Extinction?

Here is the final contrast. Are we as human persons destined for a happy heaven (or some glorious extinction) or are we destined for an eternal heaven (or an eternal hell)? In the world, there are some people who do not believe in an afterlife. They believe that when you die, you're done and that is it. Christopher Hitchens, the famous atheist who has now met his Maker, said:

I'm here as a product of the process of evolution, which doesn't make very many exceptions. And which rates life relatively cheaply. . . . I mean, most human beings who've ever been born would have been dead long before they reach my age. . . . So to be relatively healthy at sixty-two [though he soon died of cancer] is to be dealt a pretty good hand by the cosmos, which doesn't know I'm here—and won't notice when I'm gone. So that seemed to be the only properly stoic attitude to take.[14]

You see, that is it. We are here for a while, and the cosmos has given us a few years, and then we will die and cease to exist.

That is not what most people in this country believe, even if they are not Christians. Most people believe in some kind of heaven, but it's not a heaven where Christ is on the throne. It is usually a heaven where *they* sit on the throne. We have all had the uncomfortable experience of being at funerals and wishing that the pastor would say something about the gospel, but it's not there. Then family members come up, speaking about the deceased who showed no interest in spiritual things or in Christ, and yet it's stated so matter-of-factly, so authoritatively, that our friend is in a better place, or that he is up there cheering on the home team, or that he is going to help fix your car and smile upon your day—these very nebulous cultural understandings of heaven. Heaven in our culture's understanding is 100 percent glory-free. It is not a place for the glory of God to dwell. It is not a place for us to reflect the glory of Christ. There is no Christ. There is no Lamb. There is no God to be its lamp. It is one unending vacation.

John Piper has written these challenging words:

14. Quoted in "Christopher Hitchens on Suffering, Beliefs and Dying," *National Public Radio*, October 29, 2010. Accessed online at http://www.npr.org/templates /story/story.php?storyId=130917506.

> If you could have heaven, with no sickness, and with all the friends you ever had on earth, and all the food you ever liked, and all the leisure activities you ever enjoyed, and all the natural beauties you ever saw, all the physical pleasures you ever tasted, and no human conflict or any natural disasters, could you be satisfied with heaven, if Christ were not there?[15]

Many of us would have to admit, "Maybe." Of course, there is no true either/or when it comes to heaven. Because the Lord is present, the curse is reversed, and he helps us to enjoy the world as it was meant to be enjoyed. But you see the point.

Mitch Albom wrote a book a few years ago called *Five People You Will Meet in Heaven*,[16] which tells of an elderly man's conversations with five people once he dies and goes to the afterlife. In his review of the book for the *New York Times*, David Brooks described this heaven as "nothing more than an excellent therapy session" in which "friends and helpers come and tell you how innately wonderful you are." Brooks, who is not a Christian, concludes, "In this heaven, God and his glory are not the center of attention. It's all about you."[17]

The truth is that you and I are immortal, and we will live in eternal death or eternal life. Jesus tells a parable in Mark 13, warning us to be on guard and keep awake. He says that life is like a man on a journey, and the doorman must stay awake. He says, "Be on guard, keep awake. For you do not know when the time will come" (Mark 13:33). What matters now most of

15. John Piper, *God Is the Gospel: Meditations on God's Love as the Gift of Himself* (Wheaton, IL: Crossway, 2011), 15.

16. Mitch Albom, *The Five People You Meet in Heaven* (New York: Hachette Books, 2006).

17. David Brooks, "Hooked on Heaven Lite," *New York Times*, March 9, 2004, available online at http://www.nytimes.com/2004/03/09/opinion/hooked-on-heaven -lite.html.

all is what will matter later. That is the one reality of human existence that we cannot avoid: the reality of death and the judgment of God.

The Belgic Confession, Article 37, talks about heaven and hell, with a little aside that has always struck me. It speaks of the idle words that will be judged by God, "which the world regards as only playing games." Yes, the people of the world play games and are happy to keep doing so. They are happy to have a smart phone that will keep their mind off of eternal things—whatever it takes. And the sad thing is that too many churches decide that if this is what people want, then Christians can play games too. But maybe what people want is not what they really need.

In his famous sermon "Sinners in the Hands of an Angry God," Jonathan Edwards presented a startling image of the Almighty holding people over the pit of hell like a spider dangling from a web, which just a singe of flame would cut, hurtling them into the abyss. It was said that some of the people who heard that sermon could be seen lifting their feet off the ground, lest they fall into that abyss—so arresting was his image, and so striking was their fear of the wrath of God. But of course, as Christians, we do not have to fear the wrath of God because we know the One who has paid for our sins. And the heaven that awaits us is so much better, richer, higher, sweeter, safer, holier, and more glorious than any pale substitute that will find its way onto the best-seller list.

Think about the description of heaven on earth in books like Isaiah and Revelation, or in Jesus' parables or Paul's epistles. It is just staggering. There is reward, inheritance, blessing, rule, feasting, and security. There is no pain, mourning, disappointment, struggle, or fear. You won't have arthritis. You won't get canker sores. You won't have that cough. And you won't sin. Aren't you looking forward to being done with sin? You won't keep snapping like you always have. You won't keep worrying like you've been so prone to worry throughout your life. And you won't keep having that irritability with your spouse. You won't have that addiction that you struggle to break free from. There will be a celebration, a tree of life, living water, manna from heaven, unending light, and unceasing worship. Heaven is like that rare moment that you may have now when you know in your bones that God is with you, and you know that he loves you, and you want to sing and shout and tell everyone how you feel. But in heaven that moment will never end. Life everlasting is like all of the power, beauty, delight, truth, and sweetness that you can conceive of in having children and grandchildren, and vacationing at a lake or in the mountains, with laughter and good food and drink, and you roll all of that into one experience and put at the center the Lord Jesus Christ, the all-worthy One, the all-glorious One, and then you multiply that experience by ten thousand, and it never ends.

People out there just want to go somewhere where they can eat chocolate cake and have a great big therapy session and learn how important they really were. That is what C. S. Lewis meant when he said we are not asking for too much but instead "are too easily pleased." We are like, Lewis said, "an ignorant child who wants to go on making mud-pies in a slum because he cannot imagine what is meant by the offer of a holiday at the sea."[18]

On earth, all our joy is fleeting. Food tastes good, and then it is gone—except on your hips. Kids are precious, but they drive you nuts—and just about the time you like them and they like you, they leave. Then they have your grandkids, only to move somewhere far away. Our joy is always mingled with pain. Our delight is always punctuated by suffering—but not in heaven.

18. C. S. Lewis, "The Weight of Glory," in *The Weight of Glory and Other Addresses* (1949; repr., New York: HarperCollins, 2009) 26.

There glory, delight, and love are always growing, always swelling, always increasing. Every Tuesday is better than Monday. Every Wednesday is better than Tuesday. There is nonstop, continuous, everlasting glory. It is your best life later.

That is the hope. That is the aim. That is the blessedness of praising God and delighting in him forever and ever. And that is what we were made for. Created by God, fallen in Adam, redeemed by Christ, and one day glorified with all the saints, all the angels, the twenty-four elders, and the four living creatures around the throne. If only we can have our eyes opened to see who we really are and what we are really made for in this life.

4

Adam, Lord of the Garden

LIAM GOLIGHER

IN *THE SOUND OF MUSIC*, we are told to start at the very beginning; it's a very good place to start. When it comes to the Bible, we start at the end. We start with a completed canon. We start with the fulfillment of Scripture, centered on the resurrection of Jesus and looking beyond to the eternal state of the new heaven and the new earth. And when we start at the end of the book and then begin to study the rest of it, and see it in its canonical context, we discover that in the beginning our first parents enjoyed the most perfect environment. The garden of Eden becomes not simply a farm, but a sanctuary, seen from the perspective of the book of Revelation. We see Eden as a place of worship and sacred communion, a place where our first parents enjoyed a perfect relationship with the God who had made them. Moses introduced the children of Israel in the desert to the worship of Yahweh, to the tabernacle where they could not have failed to see striking resemblances to the description of Eden given in Genesis.

G. K. Beale points out a number of these resemblances.[1] Israel's temple was constructed to remember Eden, which is why it was entered from the east, guarded by cherubim, and illuminated by the menorah, the seven-branched candlestick symbolizing the tree of life. The temple was a sanctuary decorated with floral and arboreal details reminiscent of the garden. The gold and onyx we find in Eden are widely used to decorate the tabernacle and later the temple and the priestly clothing. The Lord walks in Eden and meets with man there, just as he meets with humanity in the tabernacle. The rivers that flow from Eden are like the rivers that flow from the temple, both in Ezekiel and in Revelation. The eternal state seems to be an expanded form of Eden. John writes,

> Then the angel showed me the river of the water of life, bright as crystal, flowing from the throne of God and of the Lamb through the middle of the street of the city; also, on either side of the river, the tree of life with its twelve kinds of fruit, yielding its fruit each month. The leaves of the tree were for the healing of the nations. (Rev. 22:1–2)

Ezekiel tells us that Eden is "the garden of God . . . the holy mountain of God" (Ezek. 28:13–14). He refers to the sanctuaries (v. 18), a word later used of Israel's tabernacle and temple.

Adam as King, Priest, and Prophet

So here is the perfect environment. It is designed to fulfill every one of man's needs, but in it above all man can experience

---

1. For the seminal treatment of Eden in its relationship to Israel's temple, see G. K. Beale, *The Temple and the Church's Mission: A Biblical Theology of the Dwelling Place of God* (Downers Grove, IL: InterVarsity Press, 2004).

a personal relationship with his Maker, his Creator and Provider. The garden is a perfect environment, and in it, at the apex of all God's works and at the climax to creation, is man, created by a direct act of God as the result of a decision made within the triune Godhead: "Let us make man in our image" (Gen. 1:26). Adam, soon with Eve, is placed in a wonderful environment, enjoys an intimate relationship with God, and is given a number of privileges. He is given, first of all, a royal status. He is made in the image of God. As the first Israelites heard that, they would have thought of the realities of the world around them, the world of Egypt and Mesopotamia, where the king was often described as the image and likeness of the god of that region, and where kings themselves would set up images of themselves in remote areas of their kingdom to remind people in whose territory they lived. Not only that, but we are told in the book of Revelation that in the final state, which is described in Edenic terms, the river of the water of life flows from the throne of God into the midst of the garden-city (Rev. 22:2). In other words, as in the tabernacle, where the ark of the covenant was regarded as the footstool of the invisible throne of God, it is not surprising to find the sovereignty of God displayed here in Eden. "Let us make man in our image" (Gen. 1:26). We further read, "And God blessed them. And God said to them, 'Be fruitful and multiply and fill the earth and subdue it and have dominion over the fish of the sea and over the birds of the heavens and over every living thing that moves on the earth'" (Gen. 1:28).

Here are Adam and Eve, commissioned by God as his vice-roys. Adam is given dominion over all creatures. This gives him a royal status, a *kingly* role. This involves a delegation of God's authority. Twice in three verses, the regal status conferred on man is underlined as he is made in the image of God. As the image of God, he is God's appointed king. He is to reflect the fact that he belongs to the head King, the chief King, the King of all the universe, the King who is God himself. And when we find Adam speaking, naming and giving titles to the animals that God has made, we see a reflection of God's activity in speaking and naming the things that he has made in the creative work described in chapter 1, where he speaks and things happen. God names them, separates them, and organizes them in his creative purpose.

As the image bearers of God, Adam and Eve are commissioned to be fruitful and multiply and to fill the earth and subdue it. Later on in Genesis, we find that the offspring of Adam are made in his image. So Adam is made in the image of God and is commissioned by God to fill the earth with divine image bearers. And presumably, as he would procreate more and produce more divine image bearers, they would extend Eden until it covered the whole earth, spreading God's rule throughout the whole earth. Here we see the intended scope of Adam's royal status.

Adam is also given a sacred function, that is, a *priestly* role. In the New Jerusalem of Revelation, believers are described as kings and priests, or priestly kings, serving in God's holy temple, which is the whole earth. We have seen that God gives a kingly status to Adam, but he does something else in Genesis 2:15: "The LORD God took the man and put him in the garden of Eden to work it and keep it." The two key words here are *abad*, meaning "to serve," and *shamar*, which means "to guard." Adam is to serve and to guard in the garden. In other words, Adam's function is more than agriculture. He is more than a gardener. If Eden is a sacred space, as Genesis 2 depicts it, and if it is the place where man is to enjoy communion with God, as Genesis 3 shows that he does, then only priests are permitted to work there.

Now wherever those two words, *abad* and *shamar*, "to serve" and "to guard," are used together in the Pentateuch, they describe the duties of the Levites, the priests, in the temple. The same two words are used in 1 Kings 9:6, where the serving and the guarding refer to keeping the commands of God; in Solomon's case, his sons are to guard and keep (*shamar*) the commands of God, and they are not to go off and serve (*abad*) other gods. If they go off and serve other gods, they will be cast out (v. 7). As Adam is cast out of the garden, so they will be cast out of God's sight. In 1 Chronicles 9:17–27, Israel's priests are charged to be gatekeepers, to watch (*shamar*) at the gates, so that no one can enter who is in any way unclean. In Genesis 3:24, the cherubim are stationed at the gates of Eden to guard (*shamar*) the entrance and stop people from coming in after the fall and defiling the holy place. In other words, the language of serving and guarding is used of a priestly role: to guard the holy place, to serve God in that holy place, to keep out all that is unclean from that holy place, so that it does not defile God's temple or bring down God's kingdom. In Deuteronomy 5:12, the same verb *shamar* is used to warn Israelites to guard the sanctity of the Sabbath day.

Adam is also given a prophetic word. In addition to being a king and priest, Adam is to be a *prophet*. There is the command of God in Genesis 2:16–17.

> The LORD God commanded the man, saying, "You may surely eat of every tree of the garden, but of the tree of the knowledge of good and evil you shall not eat, for in the day that you eat of it you shall surely die."

Adam should have guarded this command of God, just as one of the responsibilities of the priests of Israel was to guard the commandments of God. He should have proclaimed this word of God to his image bearers, to his descendants. He should have been a faithful spokesman of the truth of God to those who would follow after him.

The great tragedy of Adam's fall is that he fails to fulfill his prophetic mission. He is a spokesman. He is the first prophet of God in the Bible, charged to explain, proclaim, and interpret the excellencies of God by keeping intact the word of God to him and to his image bearers. He is the first priest who enjoys special access to God, serving in the sanctuary of God and charged to keep out of that holy space anything that defiles it and that is unclean. And he is the first king charged to govern in righteousness and integrity, to point away from himself to the great King, the one who made everything and who made him in his own image and likeness. As the Westminster Confession of Faith says, "They received a command, not to eat of the tree of the knowledge of good and evil; which while they kept, they were happy in their communion with God, and had dominion over the creatures" (WCF 4.2).

Adam as Covenantal Representative

In addition to serving as—in classic Reformed terms— prophet, priest, and king, Adam is given a covenantal role. The New Testament leads us to understand that God always deals with people in covenantal terms. Some make a lot of the fact that the word *covenant* is not used in Genesis 2—as it is not used initially, for example, in the covenant with David. It is not used here presumably because it would have been an anachronism to use a word that was current in Moses' day of this relationship back then. But anyone familiar with the covenants in Moses' day would have immediately recognized all the contours and the shape of a covenantal relationship. Also at this stage, of course, there is no fall. Therefore, the relationship that later has to become much more formal, having to be fenced around with formalities due to the entrance of sin, takes on a different shape. But make no mistake, Adam's role is covenantal.

This covenant is an intimate bond forged between God and his servant Adam. This relationship is unilateral in the sense that God is the one who initiates it. Adam comes with nothing to contribute to God. In all the suzerainty treaties with which Israel would have been familiar by the time Genesis was being written and taught to them by Moses, it is the great king who establishes the terms. There in the garden there is no bantering, no bartering, no bargaining, and no contracting. God comes and imposes the terms of the relationship on Adam, whom he has made, because the parties to this bond are unequal. Man is on the receiving end of extravagant generosity, surrounded by a good creation, bristling with good gifts, living well on God's terms, and enjoying remarkable fellowship with God the Father, Son, and Holy Spirit, who had made him in the image of God. "God blessed them," we read in Genesis 1:28. "And God said to them, 'Be fruitful and multiply and fill the earth and subdue it and have dominion over the fish of the sea and over the birds of the heavens and over every living thing that moves on the earth.'" Here is a statement of divine blessing that goes with the covenantal bond. There is a title to land, the whole earth. There is the prize. There is the promise. The whole earth is to be filled with human seed. There is the mandate. The whole earth is to be taken over and is to be peopled by human seed. It is a unilateral covenant relationship.

It is also a formal relationship in the sense that the declaration of the character of the bond that has been established is verbalized. The sovereign Lord, the great King, dictates the terms of the covenant. He speaks graciously to commit himself to his creatures. He declares the basis on which that relationship exists. God is never casual or informal in the relationship he establishes with man, but he is kind. He is good. He is generous. He places limits on the continuance of this relationship. There is just one simple law. It is almost embarrassingly simple. The requirement is such a small thing, it seems. From the perspective of our multiple thousands of years of human sinning, this seems such a small thing. But from the very beginning, God makes it clear that this covenant relationship that he has with humanity in Adam is a matter of life and death.

Some object to this idea of a covenantal relationship because they say the promissory aspect is only implied and is not explicit. It is implied by the reference to the tree of life, but it is not explicit because it is going to be a matter of no consequence in just a few minutes of reading the story. Adam is going to sin. What is signified by the tree of life, in a sense, is suspended. In the trajectory of the Bible, we are left there wondering what would have happened if Adam had been admitted to the tree of life. And it isn't until the end of the book that we discover what is involved in being admitted to the tree of life. It means having eternal life. It means a resurrection body. It means a new heavens and a new earth. It means the transformation of the whole universe by the power of God. For now, what might have been is left unaddressed.

The covenant bond is not only formal but also personal. As subsequent events go on to show, God pursues this relationship with Adam through abundant gifts, regular meetings, and intimate conversations. Words are important from the very outset. God speaks to man; man speaks to God. The relationship between God and man, between God and Adam, is a verbal, speaking relationship of interaction, understanding, and communication. In the end, the failure of humanity will be a breech of a command, an act of sheer ingratitude for generosity shown in the rejection of a loving and familiar Friend.

This first relationship will shape all future relationships between God and Adam's progeny. All future covenants will be variations of this most basic one. There is no period of history after Adam in which God does not deal with men and women in a covenantal way. The New Testament parallels between Adam and Christ imply that Christ was the federal head or covenant representative of the new covenant in the way that Adam was of the initial covenant. Genesis 2 and 3 teach us that Adam in Eden is a covenant mediator. He is called and empowered to bear the image of God and to mediate God's rule to creation. There is God. There is creation. And there is Adam.

In this relationship that is personal, formal, and unilaterally initiated by God, there are moral elements. Man is free to obey God with one stipulation, the probationary command given to this image bearer of God. Here is a man at the very pinnacle of genetic perfection. Women today can only dream of such a man! He is at the pinnacle—man as the image bearer of God. The tree is good. It belongs exclusively to God. The prohibition against eating from the tree of the knowledge of good and evil is intended to be a moral stimulus, not a stumbling stone. Adam, unlike those who will come after him, is in a state of rectitude, perfectly capable of obeying this law, which is not cumbersome. It is not a terribly confining or restricting law. He can have everything, including the whole earth. Everything is his, except this one thing. And the command of God is laced with love, set in the context of a personal relationship, built on the foundation of a generous provision. In this favorable circumstance, Paul tells us, Adam was acting as a covenant representative and the corporate head of humanity.

Augustine refers to Adam as "that man who first sinned and in whom we all died and from whom we were all born into a condition of misery."[2] Augustine further writes, "The first covenant was this, unto Adam: 'Whensoever thou eatest thereof, thou shalt die the death.'"[3] This is why all of us, his children, are breakers of God's covenant made with Adam in Paradise.

This first covenant was a covenant of works: if you don't eat it, you live; if you eat it, you die. It was quite straightforward and uncomplicated. If Adam had obeyed, he would have gone on, presumably, to have children for hundreds and hundreds of years, filling the earth with divine image bearers. He would have instructed them in the word of God. God's word would have been passed on, and they would have listened to it. Eden would have been extending its boundaries until it covered the whole earth, and the earth would have been filled with the knowledge of the Lord. And then, presumably, at some point Adam and his progeny would have been granted access to the tree of life, given transformed, glorious bodies like our Lord's glorious body, and the whole earth would have been glorified in order to perfectly suit eternal beings. Maybe that's what could have been, but that was not to be, because in Genesis 3 we find something else entering creation.

Adam's Fall into Sin

As we follow Adam's story, it is vital to underline that it takes place in a good creation. There is no blip to the goodness. There is no crease in the perfect smoothness of humanity's response

2. Augustine, *Confessions*, trans. Henry Chadwick (Oxford: Oxford University Press, 1991), 196–97.
3. Augustine, *City of God*, 16.27.

to God. It is a good creation. So when sin appears, it appears as an intruder in the garden. There is no eternal struggle between good and evil in the Bible. Evil is not inherent to matter. It is not part of the universe. Evil is not a necessary component of the material and physical world. Nor does sin belong to the very essence of human nature. People today who think that Adam was some kind of tribal chieftain whom God selected and chose to use ignore the fact that this means there was sin and evil before Adam, because there was death before him. And that means that sin is built into the very nature of humanity. But in the Bible's account, sin is an alien intruder. It is a historical disruption, deep in the history of mankind's experience of God's good world. Sin is not normal, but an anomaly. It is a gate crasher, an intruder. In Ezekiel 28:13–14, the prophet situates Eden, the garden of God, on God's holy mountain, and Eden's name says it all: it is a delight, a place of pleasure. It is the epitome of happiness. It is the gift that leaves nothing to be desired, with man and nature in perfect harmony. That is the context in which Adam sins. There are no excuses for his behavior.

Today bad behavior is usually explained away because of heredity, environment, upbringing, circumstances, health, or life experiences. But here we return to the river of humanity, back to Adam, humanity at its purest source. He is the finest flower of genetic material. He is the perfect person, in the perfect environment, enjoying a perfect life. There is no excuse or accounting for what happens next.

Augustine says that Adam had two abilities. First, he was *posse peccare*, able to sin. Second, Adam was *posse non peccare*, able not to sin. Adam had the ability to sin and the ability not to sin. Augustine also says that our first parents were *posse mori*, able to die, and *posse non mori*, able not to die. So they were not created immortal. That is the significance of the tree of life. They could die under certain circumstances, but death was not necessary to Adam and Eve. Had they obeyed God's commandments, they would not have died.

Coming to Genesis 3, we discover that the tempter implicitly threatens the word of God. He does so by his very presence in the garden. Adam and Eve have been given dominion over all the animals, and now here is an animal leading Eve and then Adam into a discussion about God and then leading them into sin. There is an implicit contradiction of their covenant relationship with God. Here is an inversion of the order of creation. Man is supposed to have dominion over everything else, as the image bearer of God. But here is an animal overriding an image bearer of God, and here is a wife leading her husband. This is no casual or innocent conversation.

As soon as the conversation begins, the word of God is under threat. Already they are failing to keep and guard the garden. Disaster is in the making. Man, who was given dominion over the animals, is going to yield to an animal and fall into sin. The consequence of this event throughout the rest of Scripture is immense. The fall involves a complete inversion of the creation order. Thus, when man creates for himself gods of his own imagination, he often pictures them as animals. He bows to them. He makes his sacrifices to animal images. As the priest charged with guarding the garden, ensuring that foreign elements do not enter and disrupt and destroy, Adam has failed to guard the garden of God.

Similarly in the New Testament, Christian leaders are responsible for guarding the gospel and the church. The foreign elements that insinuate sin into the church and that insinuate false teaching into the church have to be recognized, identified, and excluded from the church. We cannot play around with it. The charge to New Testament elders is to guard the church of God.

Once in the garden, the tempter implicitly threatens the word of God by casting doubt upon it. John Calvin writes,

> Let us pay close attention to how sin entered and how the devil caught Eve and Adam off guard. There are two ports of entry. Two ears which received Satan's voice . . . [Therefore] what must be done? Evil must be repaired in the same way. Our two ears must listen to God's Word and that Word must enter us in a living way and dwell there and fortify us in such a way that the devil cannot get in.[4]

The serpent appears out of nowhere. He speaks like a winsome, angelic theologian. He maneuvers Eve into a sincere theological discussion, beginning by raising a question: "Did God actually say, 'You shall not eat of any tree in the garden'?" (Gen. 3:1). His approach is subtle. "Did God really say? Did he actually say this?" He is raising a question about the veracity, sincerity, and trustworthiness of God's word. He is raising doubt about God's character, his truthfulness. And then, on the pretense of having merely a theological discussion, he stresses the prohibition and not God's provision. "Did God actually say, 'You shall not eat of *any* tree in the garden'?" Theological professors are still using the same technique to lead their students into error today.

Eve is quick, however. She sets the serpent straight. She tells him that God has given them free use of the garden, with one exception. Only one tree is off limits, while the rest are theirs to enjoy. The serpent gets her to express the command in her own words, rather than in God's. Here Eve learns the first lesson that every pastor and Sunday school

4. John Calvin, *Sermons on Genesis: Chapters 1–11*, ed. Rob Roy McGregor (Edinburgh: Banner of Truth Trust, 2009), 235.

teacher needs to learn: you do not paraphrase when you are quoting God.

I recently attended a church in London that I know quite well. I had heard that the new pastor was very keen on communicating with people today. His challenge is that people in England today do not understand biblical language anymore. They do not know, for instance, that the word *hallowed* means "holy." So when the pastor was leading the Lord's Prayer, he used the word *honored* in the place of "hallowed." But *honored* is a different word than *hallowed*! I was astonished at his willingness to change even Jesus' words, apparently with little concern for the consequences.

The serpent got Eve to restate what God had said, and in doing so, she began to waiver. She began to yield to the serpent's denials and half-truths by adding to the prohibition "neither shall you touch it" (Gen. 3:3). But God had not said that. In this way, Eve became the first legalist. Then she lessened the warning against sin from "you shall surely die" to "lest you die" (Gen. 2:17; 3:3). Thus she became the first theological liberal. Notice the tempter's skill in covertly questioning the word of God, a skill he practices widely today.

Only now does the tempter overtly contradict God's Word. He has the advantage, having subtly created a fissure in Eve's thinking, and into that slight fissure he puts his lever and cranks the fissure open. Into that opening he places the lie: "You will not surely die" (Gen. 3:4). He seeks to comfort her fears. But in comforting her fears, he directly contradicts the word of God.

Did you know that we tend to do this in pastoral counseling? We do this in conversation with a friend who is not a Christian or who is hostile to the things of God. We cannot bear that they should fall out with us or think we are narrow, difficult, or awkward people. So we water down God's Word. We crank down the terms. It is exactly this that Satan did to Eve, so as to effect Adam's downfall.

Finally comes Satan's *coup de grâce*: "God knows that when you eat of it your eyes will be opened, and you will be like God, knowing good and evil" (Gen. 3:5). This is a lie big enough to reinterpret the whole of life: "God does not want you to know what he knows. He does not want you to fulfill your potential. He is afraid of you. You will know something that God does not want you to know." And here is the key: what attracted Eve was knowledge. At the end of the day, it is what she could know that is more attractive than eating the fruit. There is knowledge that has been withheld from her, knowledge that would change the world for her. Not only that, but Satan makes the command of God into something wicked and greedy, low and mean. He wants her to think badly of God. He charges God with a kind of jealousy. God does not want your eyes opened. He does not want you to reach his level of knowledge. Satan wants Eve to feel as if God is holding back from her something that would enhance her humanity and make her feel better about herself and the world and complete her and satisfy her. How many of us fall into sin because we believe that lie? If only she would take the fruit, she would realize her destiny. She would become like God.

What the serpent is doing, of course, is reinterpreting all of life. He is putting his word against God's word. He is saying that God's rules are unfair. Man has the inalienable right to do as he pleases, even if it is not pleasing to God. That thought process goes on in human minds every day.

Notice the anomaly in this. Here is Eve talking to the serpent. She does not know the serpent from Adam's pussycat. She has never met this serpent before. She has known God all her life, however long that has been by this stage. Here is this strange intruder, and she is listening to him! In Genesis 3, Satan's challenge to God's word is an opportunity for Adam and Eve to step up to the plate and to defend God's authority. They could say, "Wait a second, we serve the Lord God of heaven and earth, who made us, and we are his image bearers! We serve him. We believe him implicitly. And if you don't believe him implicitly, get out of the garden!" And notice that the first doctrine that is ever denied explicitly is the doctrine of divine judgment, just as Satan still downplays the gravity of sin. We are still temped to think that God's bark is worse than his bite, that he is not quite as holy as the Scriptures say he is. The modern denial of God's judgment and wrath in hell is nothing new.

In describing this situation, Paul tells us that Eve was deceived (1 Tim. 2:14). That is how we are to understand the expression "when the woman saw" (Gen. 3:6). The verb *to see* is being used in the way we use it when we say, "I see your point." It is knowledge that she wants, not food. Se is hungry for the power that comes from knowledge, because knowledge has a potential for evil as well as good. Eve is anxious to have that knowledge.

Temptation plays with the mind, you see, to gain knowledge that makes us look wise. It's interesting, isn't it, that we don't normally think of temptation as an assault on reason or on the mind. Usually, when we talk about temptation, we think much lower in the anatomy than the brain and the mind. But you see the point that's being made here. Eve let this creature get her thinking independently of God's revelation, thinking that she could think and act independently of God's revealed, spoken word. That is where temptation begins and assaults us today. The failure to believe God, when God has spoken, is at the root of all sin. The failure simply to believe God is to be guilty of slandering his righteous character. It is an assault on his integrity. And at the end of the day, that is why Adam sinned. Adam refused to believe God, and he fell.

This means that if you and I want to see sin in its most basic form, we should not look at the crack house or the bordello; we should look at the academy and the seminary, to the opinion formers and the media pundits, because fundamentally sin is an assault on the truth of God. All truth is God's truth, but God's revealed truth stands above all other sources of truth available to humanity. So when scholars say that the academic consensus requires us to believe in evolution, contrary to the clear teaching of God's Word, they are falling for the lie of the Devil.

The Promise of a Second Adam

We need to remind ourselves that the Great Commission that God gave to Adam in Genesis 1 involves more than simply procreating. It means filling the earth with image bearers who reflect God's glory and obey the command of God that was given as a key to doing this. If they had obeyed, their children would have been raised in the instruction of God's word, and on they would have gone to fill the earth and to subdue it. In Colossians 1:10, Paul uses terminology from Genesis 1:28, speaking of the word of truth and the gospel "bearing fruit . . . and increasing" in the world. This is the way that Adam was told to bear fruit, increase, and multiply. Similarly, we see in the book of Acts that it is the Word of God that leads the church to bear fruit, increase, and multiply until it reaches the ends of the earth. In other words, the gospel commission today is the commission given to Adam. It involves the multiplication of image bearers, people who are being renewed in the image of Christ, who is himself the image of the invisible God. And as image bearers, born again by the Spirit of God, capture the Word of God in their hearts, and as their influence spreads around the globe to more and more people, the Word of God multiplies and abounds and becomes fruitful, and more and more people embrace the Lord Jesus by the grace of God.

But the solemn thing for us is that it was by doubting God and not defending his word that this first couple sinned. Eve took and ate. There was doubt, dissatisfaction, desire, and deception. In Adam's case, there was the addition of sheer disobedience. As our covenant mediator, he failed us. And so Paul gives us the interpretation of the story: "Sin came into the world through one man, and death through sin, and so death spread to all men because all sinned" (Rom. 5:12). You cannot escape the covenantal and corporate rule of Adam as the representative of all humanity and all creation. And it is the story of Adam that sets us up for the human story that unfolds, except that a most remarkable thing happens. Instead of the penalty being immediately effected, Adam's death is held back for several hundred years. Instead of the sentence being read out, a promise is made. It is a unilateral promise. This time there is no *if.* It is an absolute promise. The penalty is put in suspense. And the promise is made that there will be enmity between Satan and the woman: "I will put enmity between you and the woman, and between your offspring and her offspring; he shall bruise your head, and you shall bruise his heel" (Gen. 3:15). God initiates conflict between Satan's offspring and the woman's offspring, and, like two armed camps, their respective lines will be engaged in mortal combat. And then he announces that "he" (singular), the offspring of the woman, will crush "your" (Satan's) head; and you, Satan, will strike his heel. From two opposing armies, it will come down to two warring individuals in hand-to-hand mortal combat—one representing the hardened host of hell, and the other representing the redeemed host of God.

> O loving wisdom of our God!
> When all was sin and shame,
> A second Adam to the fight
> And to the rescue came.[5]

5. John H. Newman, "Praise to the Holiest in the Height," 1865.

5

The Bible and Evolution

RICHARD D. PHILLIPS

*Then the LORD God formed the man of dust from
the ground and breathed into his nostrils the breath
of life, and the man became a living creature.*
(Genesis 2:7)

STARTING IN 1610, Galileo Galilei published a series of
books that brought him into conflict with the Roman Catholic
Church. His books endorsed the heliocentric theory of Coper-
nicus, which stated that the sun was the center of the solar
system and that the earth rotated around the sun. At that time,
the church insisted on the centrality of the earth, based on its
interpretation of Joshua 10:13, in which God caused the sun to
stop in the sky in order to give Israel time to destroy its enemies
in battle. According to the church, a literal reading of the Bible
required the belief that the sun moves across the sky and, hence,

that the earth is stationary at the center of the universe. In 1633, Galileo was tried on a heresy charge for teaching the centrality of the sun, resulting in his house arrest for the remainder of his life.

The story of Galileo is retold today as a warning against religious superstition in opposition to scientific truth. Among many evangelicals today, the conflict between Galileo and the church on heliocentricity offers a parallel that may remove the barrier to the Christian acceptance of evolution. After all, it is said, unless you believe that the sun revolves around the earth—a view clearly disproved by space exploration—then you must see this as an instance in which biblical teaching was corrected by scientific evidence. This point is deemed of vital importance, since many people today live with such confidence in scientific findings that it constitutes an obstacle to embracing a Christian faith that rejects evolution. Since virtually every non-Christian in the twenty-first century seems to believe in evolution, the Christian denial of it gives us the appearance of the ostrich with its head in the sand. Old Testament scholar Bruce Waltke stated, "If the data is overwhelmingly in favor of evolution, to deny that reality will make us a cult . . . some odd group that is not really interacting with the world."[1]

Whereas secularists use the Galileo story to urge the rejection of the Bible in favor of science, pro-evolution Christians take a different tack. They correctly point out that the church was wrong about the earth and the sun only because it misinterpreted the Bible's teaching in Joshua 10:13. When that verse speaks of the sun stopping in the sky, they argue, it presents the situation from the viewer's point of view. The purpose of the verse is to show how God enabled Israel to triumph, not to argue for the centrality of the earth in the solar system. Likewise, they urge,

1. Bruce Waltke, "Why Must the Church Come to Accept Evolution?," *BioLogos*, March 24, 2010, http://biologos.org/blog/why-must-the-church-come-to-accept-evolution.

the scientific consensus on evolution reveals errors in how we have interpreted the account of creation in Genesis. The more honest of these proponents of evolution recognize that the embrace of evolution will require some shifts in various theological positions. Peter Enns writes that "evolution cannot simply be grafted onto evangelical Christian faith as an add-on. . . . This is going to take some work—and a willingness to take theological risk . . . a willingness to rethink one's own convictions in light of new data."[2]

In this chapter, I want to probe these matters. Does the theory of evolution expose errors in our interpretation of Genesis? Is it possible to maintain a high view of biblical authority and embrace evolution? Most important, what kind of theology, and what kind of Christianity, do we end up with after we have incorporated evolutionary teaching into our theology?

Evolution versus Biblical Authority

It is frankly admitted by supporters of evolution that anything like a literal reading of Genesis 1 rules out evolutionary theory. The chapter's entire scheme of creation is alien to naturalistic evolution. Here we see that God created the creatures by means of direct, special creation: "God created the great sea creatures and every living creature that moves, with which the waters swarm, according to their kinds, and every winged bird according to its kind" (Gen. 1:21). The "kinds" are the various species, which did not evolve one from another, but were each

2. Peter Enns, "Evangelism and Evolution ARE in Serious Conflict (and that's not the end of the world)," *Patheos*, January 21, 2012, http:// http://www.patheos .com/blogs/peterenns/2012/01/evangelicalism-and-evolution-are-in-serious -conflict-and-that%E2%80%99s-not-the-end-of-the-world. See also Peter Enns, *The Evolution of Adam: What the Bible Does and Doesn't Say about Human Origins* (Grand Rapids: Brazos Press, 2012), 147.

specially created by God. The land animals were created "according to their kinds" (Gen. 1:25), and this is especially true of the highest creature, man: "God created man in his own image, . . . male and female he created them" (Gen. 1:27). Thus, according to Tim Keller, to "account for evolution we must see at least Genesis 1 as non-literal."[3]

To believe in the Bible and accept evolution, then, we must remove the obstacle that Genesis 1 poses. The chief strategy for doing this is to declare that Genesis 1 functions as poetry rather than history. Since Genesis 1 uses highly stylized language and a repetitive structure, it is argued, the chapter should be considered a semi-poetic narrative. Keller asserts that Genesis 1 is like the Song of Miriam in Exodus 15 or the Song of Deborah in Judges 5. It corresponds in general to what happened, but it is a mainly poetic rendition that must not be taken as teaching literal history. Genesis 2, which is deemed the more literal creation account, is considered to present a naturalistic progression more in keeping with science. In contrast to Genesis 2, Genesis 1's supernaturalism is said to rule it out as teaching "the actual processes by which God created human life."[4]

An evaluation of this view shows that this case against the historicity of Genesis 1 is remarkably weak. Genre analysis looks for literary patterns that reflect a certain type of literature. It turns out that Genesis 1 is a classic example not of Hebrew poetry, but of Old Testament historical narrative. "This happened and then this happened and then this happened"—that is the structure of historical narrative as clearly seen in Genesis 1. Hebrew poetry relies on parallelism, yet even the repetitions of Genesis 1 do

3. Tim Keller, "Creation, Evolution, and Christian Laypeople," *BioLogos*, accessed December 22, 2014, http://biologos.org/uploads/projects/Keller_white _paper.pdf, 2.
4. Ibid., 5.

not fit this poetical pattern. Normally, if a biblical passage has the grammatical structure of historical narrative, it is treated as a historical account. But some do not interpret Genesis 1 this way, because that would conflict with the demands of secular science. Genesis 1 is compared to the Song of Miriam in Exodus 15 as a poetic expression of historical events that conveys meaning, but not necessarily literal facts. But consider the actual data of Exodus 15:

> I will sing to the LORD, for he has triumphed gloriously;
>   the horse and his rider he has thrown into the sea.
> The LORD is my strength and my song,
>   and he has become my salvation;
> this is my God, and I will praise him,
>   my father's God, and I will exalt him. (Ex. 15:1–2)

This is Hebrew poetry, to be sure. Let us then read from Genesis 1:

> In the beginning, God created the heavens and the earth. The earth was without form and void, and darkness was over the face of the deep. And the Spirit of God was hovering over the face of the waters. (Gen. 1:1–2)

This is not at all like the Song of Miriam, or the Song of Deborah in Judges 5. This is a straightforward account of one event following after another—a historical record.

The genre of Genesis 1 is the same as the genre of Genesis 2 through 50: historical narrative. Therefore, the arguments used to remove the historicity of Genesis 1 must inevitably be used against the whole of Genesis and all its teaching about God and man that is opposed to secularist dogma, including the fall of mankind, Noah's flood, the Tower of Babel, the destruction of

Sodom and Gomorrah, and God's covenant of salvation with Abraham. Once we accept that biblical narratives that sound strange to modern ears, or that have some commonality with ancient Near Eastern writings, are to be considered as myth, there is no legitimate basis to isolate this procedure to the first three or the first eleven chapters of the Bible.

The agenda of those who seek to make evolution compatible with the Bible reaches its height in their analysis of Genesis 2:7, the key verse that describes God's creation of Adam: "Then the LORD God formed the man of dust from the ground and breathed into his nostrils the breath of life, and the man became a living creature." Keller cites approvingly a theory proposed by Derek Kidner, which suggests that this may be highly figurative language that refers to mankind evolving from more primitive species over millions of years of evolutionary processes.[5] In response, we must point out that one would never get this idea from the text of Genesis 2:7 itself. The only way to get evolution out of Genesis 2:7 is first to put evolution into Genesis 2:7. This interpretation does not grant authority to the Bible, but submits the biblical text to the apparently higher authority of secularist dogma.

The attempt to show that the Bible, when properly interpreted, makes allowance for evolution simply does not work. The testimony of the Bible for a divine creation that rules out evolution is simply too direct and clear. For this reason, Christian proponents of evolution must ultimately subordinate the authority of God's Word to the authority of secularist dogma and scientific theory. Jack Collins has stated, for instance, that if the Human Genome Project were to show conclusively that human DNA cannot be traced to a single pair of humans, Christians might have to revise their beliefs about Adam.[6] Perhaps he

5. Derek Kidner, *Genesis* (Chicago: InterVarsity Press, 1967), 28.
6. C. John Collins, *Did Adam and Eve Really Exist?* (Wheaton: Crossway, 2011), 120.

would have to be considered one of a group of proto-humans who was selected to be the titular head. Perhaps Adam would be seen as head of a tribal confederation among early mankind. In principle, this approach subordinates the authority of God's Word to the authority of secular science.

This contradiction between evolution and the Bible's teaching is the first reason why Christians must reject the secularist dogma of evolution, even though this rejection may scandalize us before the world: to embrace evolution is to sacrifice the authority of the Bible. Psalm 19 says, "The testimony of the LORD is sure, making wise the simple; the precepts of the LORD are right, rejoicing the heart" (Ps. 19:7–8). The attempts to remove the testimony of Genesis 1, accommodate the teaching of Genesis 2, and marginalize the rest of the Bible's affirmations of these passages do not represent valid interpretations of the Scriptures. The only way to accept evolution is to place the Bible under the authority of secular demands, the result of which can only be the eradication of Christian teaching on sin and salvation, along with the Christian view of morality and life.

Evolution versus Biblical Humanity

If the first casualty of a Christian embrace of evolution is the authority of Scripture, the second casualty must inevitably be the biblical doctrine of man. A previous chapter explained that the biblical doctrine of creation grants dignity and value to mankind as the unique pinnacle of God's creation, made specially in the image of God. Under evolution, man's unique standing is shaken: he is not above the animals, but rather is one of them. Genesis 2:7 says that God made man with unique personal involvement, employing his own hands and creating man for face-to-face intimacy with his Maker. Evolution says that man evolved incrementally from lower forms of animals to our current position, which is itself merely a step in our upward biological climb to a higher state.

The evolutionary doctrine of man runs into conflict with the teaching of Psalm 8, for instance. There David says that God created man in a mediating position between the angels and the lower created beings: "You have made him a little lower than the heavenly beings and crowned him with glory and honor" (Ps. 8:5). Notice that David believed that God "made" mankind. God did not create a lower form of animal that then evolved into man, so that Adam emerged from the beasts; rather, God created man above the beasts and gave him dominion over them. Notice, as well, that while Psalm 8 places man between angels and beasts, man is identified not with those below him, but with those above him. David does not say that God made man "a little above the creatures," as evolution would demand, but rather "a little lower than the heavenly beings." Man is to gain his identity not by looking downward to the beasts but by looking upward to the glorious beings of heaven, where man's destiny and calling lie. This is completely contrary to the evolutionary scheme. Psalm 8 identifies us in terms of our relationship to God. James Boice writes that this tells us "we will never understand human beings unless we see them as God's creatures and recognize that they have special responsibilities to their Creator."[7]

It would be a singular disaster at this moment in history for Christians to accept an evolutionary doctrine of mankind in which Adam is merely a slightly higher form of beast. The

7. James M. Boice, *Psalms* (Grand Rapids: Baker, 1994), 1:67.

effects of secularism have so ravaged people today that despair and self-loathing are rife. To tell people that they are slightly higher versions of chimpanzees is to direct them to a bestial approach to life, in keeping with the lower species from which we came. The Bible insists, instead, that every man or woman is a special creature designed to know God and to relate to him in covenant love and faithfulness. Looking up, we see the dignity of our position in creation and the glory of our heavenly calling. Therefore, the only way for Christians to uphold the biblical doctrine of human dignity is to reject the contrary doctrine of evolution.

Moreover, the Bible's teaching of Adam as the first man, and Adam and Eve as the first parents, is the biblical basis for the unity of the human race and the brotherhood of mankind. If there was no first set of parents from which we all derived, then we are fundamentally competitors, and the very nature of our current state of being and of our hopes for survival require the violent subjugation of those who might threaten our DNA. Evolution as a theory is compatible with racism. We are not one race, but many races, and there are higher evolutionary strands and lower evolutionary strands. Evolutionary theory implies that the weak may be dominated by the strong for the evolutionary good of the race. The value of a human being lies in his utility, not in his status as a unique creation bearing the image of God. Therefore, deformed or weakened babies may be justly eliminated, and the aged and infirmed who now merely absorb resources may be put to an early end. Under evolution, the value of a human life is based on the quality of the genes it passes on and its perceived utility to the world. It is a theory that can lead only to the barbarism that is increasingly evident in our post-Christian Western society.

Evolution versus the Bible's
Teaching on Sin and Death

According to the Bible, the great problem of this world is mankind's fall into sin through the disobedience of Adam. Romans 5:16 says that "the judgment following one trespass brought condemnation." Genesis 3 teaches that as the result of Adam's sin, our first parents were cast out from the garden, away from the tree of life, to live under God's curse for sin. Evangelical supporters of evolution argue that we may still believe the theology of the fall, but first they tell us that the key Bible passages on the fall involve persons who never existed. How, then, can the doctrine of the fall be true when the events related in Genesis 3 could not have happened and the account must therefore be understood as myth?

Under an evolutionary model, sin cannot be attributed to the historical event of the fall. Rather, man's evolutionary "creation" was defective in a way that natural selection was bound to improve. This is fundamentally different from the biblical account of sin and of the great problem of the world. This difference is to be expected, since evolution is a fundamentally different grand narrative of history from that presented in the Bible. Evolution demands the abandonment of the grand biblical narrative of creation, fall, and redemption for a narrative of gradual improvement via natural selection. The scheme of evolution grounds sin and its misery in a defect in God's creative work, which is increasingly being repaired by evolution, rather than grounding sin in the historical fall whereby Paradise was lost.

If there was no historical Adam and Eve, or if the actual historical persons were different from what the Bible says, then the story of our first parents being cast out of the garden of Eden loses its doctrinal implications. The fall becomes a metaphor for something other than the actual loss of Paradise on the basis of transgression. If sin is now conceived of as resulting from a primitive evolutionary state, then salvation must consist of progress to higher states of an evolving species. This is, of course, the secular humanist position intended to replace the Christian religion, based on evolution. Pro-evolution Christians will object to this analysis, insisting that they believe the Bible's teaching on sin. The problem is that they no longer accept the biblical basis for the Christian doctrine of sin, namely, the historical reality of Adam and Eve, their fall into sin, and God's response in justly casting them from Paradise. The doctrine hangs suspended in air, with no historical events to ground its truth.

Moreover, according to the Bible, death is the direct and judicial result of sin. Paul writes that "sin came into the world through one man, and death through sin, and so death spread to all men because all sinned" (Rom. 5:12). This is fundamentally in conflict with evolution, since evolution works by means of death. Under evolution, mankind ended up as the species he is because death eliminated more inferior alternatives via natural selection. Most Christian evolutionists argue that this was God's choice and that God shaped the way that evolution brought about our race. This means that God wields death as a primary means of bringing about what the Bible describes as creation. When God said, "And it was good," he was describing a process governed by death and in which death is crucial to that which is good. This of course calls into question the very goodness and character of God, who wields death not as a judicial response to sin and rebellion but as integral to the construction of the world that declares his glory. The mythical image of the Grim Reaper must now be considered a metaphor for God himself. It is hard to imagine a doctrine more offensive to the theology of the Bible.

For Christians to separate the vital biblical link between sin and death is to lose the very essence of our religion. The book of Leviticus includes a holiness code whereby death is cast out of Israel's camp and kept far from the presence of God. Anyone with a skin disease or an issue of blood must go away from the tabernacle because Israel's God was a God of life. God was banishing death because he would defeat it by a substitutionary atoning sacrifice. Evolution turns this on its head. Its God is a God of death, and history is an account of progress that is red in tooth and claw, not because man rebelled in sin, but because of the very evolutionary process that God himself initiated. What can the book of Revelation mean, then, when it directs our hope to a new world in which "death shall be no more" (Rev. 21:4), if the God we worship in eternity has from the beginning put his benediction on the ravages of death?

One evangelical writer who is troubled by the implication of evolution and death is Tim Keller. In his paper proposing our acceptance of evolution, Keller suggests that the fall merely brought about spiritual death, since evolution teaches bodily death as integral to the fabric of creation.[8] Physical death has always been part of God's plan, but we are to ascribe spiritual death to the fall. On this view, the loss to the Christian faith is staggering. When a man or woman stands over the bed of his mother watching her die, Christianity no longer says that this is wrong, that this is opposed to God, that this is an enemy that God has vowed to overcome and destroy. "The last enemy to be destroyed is death" (1 Cor. 15:26), says the Bible. But informed by evolution, the Christian instead thinks that only spiritual death is the result of the fall. The death of a child or parent or friend is no longer in itself a great evil opposed by

8. Keller, "Creation, Evolution, and Christian Laypeople," 12.

God. Because of the doctrine of evolution, Christians must abandon in principle our position as people of life and join the secularist culture with its callous acceptance of the fundamental necessity and virtue of death. To deny this shift is merely to avoid the implication of what the theory of evolution is: a description of human progress by means of the death of those deemed inferior. Death is the instrument by which evolution works, and it must be embraced as essentially good in the worldview shaped by evolution. A religious position more opposed to Christianity is hard to imagine.

Evolution versus the Christian Doctrine of Salvation

One of the New Testament passages most directly impacted by the embrace of evolution is Paul's grand construction of history in Romans 5:12–21. There Adam is the first man, whose fall into sin brought the human race into judgment. Adam was not only the first man, but also the prototype of the true and final man, Jesus Christ. Paul calls Adam "a type of the one who was to come" (Rom. 5:14). He grounds man's covenantal union with Adam in our ontological oneness as his actual offspring. The problem of the world is that one man sinned and "judgment following one trespass brought condemnation" (Rom. 5:16). The answer to this problem, the gospel of the Christian religion, is that Jesus Christ answered the failure of our first covenant head, Adam. Paul writes,

> Therefore, as one trespass led to condemnation for all men, so one act of righteousness leads to justification and life for all men. For as by the one man's disobedience the many were

97

made sinners, so by the one man's obedience the many will be made righteous. (Rom. 5:18–19)

According to Paul, the pattern of salvation designed by God through Jesus Christ is joined to the pattern of Adam's fall as our covenant head. The Christian doctrine of salvation is that the second Adam, Jesus Christ, has overcome the failure of the first Adam by his life of perfect righteousness and his sin-atoning death. The Christian doctrine of salvation is thus summarized by Paul:

For as by a man came death, by a man has come also the resurrection of the dead. For as in Adam all die, so also in Christ shall all be made alive. (1 Cor. 15:21–22)

The problem for evolutionists is their contention that this Adam did not exist. Or if he did exist, as more theologically astute Christians realize he must, it was not the Adam described in Genesis 1 and 2. Death did not come into the world in the way that Paul describes it in keeping with Genesis 3, for death was part of the fabric of the world from the beginning. Scholars like Peter Enns urge us to accept that Paul was simply wrong about a historical Adam, though Romans 5:12–21 should still be considered theologically true.[9] Apart from the fact that Paul is no longer a credible source of truth, this makes no sense at all. The very argument that Paul makes about Adam, sin, and death is fundamentally at odds with evolution's version of history. If this is the Bible's doctrine of salvation, it addresses a sin problem that is mythical, not historically real. On what basis may we conclude that the Christian gospel is itself anything other than another ancient myth, designed to address a problem

9. Enns, *The Evolution of Adam*, 119–35.

that we know has no connection with the world described by evolutionary science?

The theory of evolution assaults the person and work of Jesus Christ at every level. What does it mean that Jesus was true and perfect man, able on this basis to make an atoning sacrifice for the sins of many? From our perspective two thousand years later, Jesus can only have been an inferior member of our race, upon whom we now look down from our slightly superior evolutionary perch. Michael Reeves points out that the church's Christology relies on Jesus having assumed *our* nature in his incarnation. The Nicene fathers insisted that "whatever Christ did not assume in his incarnation could not be 'healed' or saved" by his redeeming work.[10] Reeves concludes, "If, however, Adam was not the progenitor of all humanity, but merely a member of one of any number of disconnected branches of *Homo sapiens*, then [this] maxim begins to look rather worrying. If Christ did not assume my flesh, but the flesh of another humanity, then he is not my kinsman-redeemer."[11]

The work of Christ, which the Bible centers on his perfect fulfilling of the demands of a divine law given first to Adam in the garden, and then on his voluntarily offering of his life to pay the penalty for the sins of those who believe in him, belongs to a different world than that described by evolution—it belongs to the world of Genesis 1–3. Were not the doctrines of penal substitutionary atonement and imputed righteousness first introduced in Genesis 3:21, when God slew innocent animals to cover the sin of Adam and Eve? What are we to make of these doctrines, if there was no Adam and Eve, or a different Adam and Eve from how the Bible tells

10. Michael Reeves, "Adam and Eve," in *Should Christians Embrace Evolution?*, ed. Norman C. Nevin (Phillipsburg, NJ: P&R Publishing, 2009), 55.
11. Ibid.

it, and thus no first, primordial sin passed on to all their offspring by natural generation?

Evolution: Small Gain and Great Loss

When we calculate the gain and loss from the Christian embrace of evolution, the results are not encouraging. By the very nature of the evolutionary theory itself, so much of the Bible's teaching, not only of creation but also of redemption, must be rethought. Man is no longer a unique, special creation designed by God for spiritual and covenant fellowship with him. Rather, we are a more advanced kind of animal, and if God has invested a special status upon us, it is not by virtue of what we are as creatures. Mankind no longer has two parents in whom we derive a common ancestry. No longer may we think of death as a heinous intrusion into God's creation, but rather as a fundamental feature of what God made and called "good." Death did not occur as the result of man's sinful rebellion against God. Christian ethics must also be fundamentally revised under evolution. Peter Enns has written, "Some behaviors that Christians have thought of as sinful are understood in an evolutionary scheme as means of ensuring survival—for example, the aggression and dominance associated with 'survival of the fittest' and sexual promiscuity to perpetuate one's gene pool."[12] Enns is right, and his candor should be appreciated. Evolution cannot be grafted onto the structure of biblical Christianity, but replaces it with a different structure, a different ethic, a different story of salvation, and a different religion altogether.

12. Enns, "Evangelism and Evolution ARE in Serious Conflict." See also Enns, *The Evolution of Adam*, 147.

I strongly doubt that most Christians who urge an embrace of evolution, or at least its tolerance, envision so staggering a loss as the result. They see a gain: no longer would Christians have to be considered anti-science ostriches with our heads in the sand. We would not have to play the role of the pope in his battle with Galileo, however weak the analogy may be between that situation and ours today. No longer would we be categorically excluded from the possibility of dialogue in the market square of secular society. No longer would we be a cult of obscurantists who refuse to accept what everyone else knows. No longer would we argue matters that seem so far removed from the good news of forgiveness through a loving Savior. With the credibility of our tolerant consideration of evolution, we would gain an opportunity to discuss Jesus as the loving Savior.

Do we realize the folly of this reasoning? The problem is that as soon as we go from evolution to the person and work of Jesus Christ, we have reverted to the narrative that began in Genesis 1, 2, and 3. The logic of the gospel we seek to present is one that belongs to the story of Adam as the special image bearer of God, who brought sin and death into the world by transgression. Moreover, the events of Christ's life that we proclaim are as unacceptable to the postmodern worldview as the special creation of Adam. We would be holding forth the doctrines of a Bible that we have already subjected to the higher authority of secularist dogma and scientific claims, neither of which will tolerate Christ's atoning death and bodily resurrection. In short, by the folly of our desire to escape the persecution of a world that does not tolerate God's Word, we have ourselves abandoned the history taught in the Bible, which alone can support the story of the Christian message, the gospel of Jesus as the Savior for our sins.

How little is the gain and how catastrophic must be the loss to a Christianity that capitulates to a narrative that is in its very essence designed to replace the teaching of God's Word regarding everything in our world. But what is the alternative, asks the anguished evangelical facing the world's demand that we conform or be excluded from its society and conversation? The biblical alternative was given by Paul: "Let God be true though every one were a liar" (Rom. 3:4). We must decide that the Bible is God's Word and therefore is the highest authority on every matter to which it speaks. James asks us pointedly today, "You adulterous people! Do you not know that friendship with the world is enmity with God? Therefore whoever wishes to be a friend of the world makes himself an enemy of God" (James 4:4). But how can we expect to reach and redeem a world if our teaching results in such an offense that we are deemed a cult of intellectual outrages, unwilling to face the truths of a modern world? We do it in the same way that the apostles and the Christians of the early church did it, by the power of God at work to save through his gospel. Paul tells us how he upheld outrageous doctrines in the midst of an ancient pagan world with its nonbiblical narrative. He writes,

> Having this ministry by the mercy of God, we do not lose heart. . . . We refuse to practice cunning or to tamper with God's word, but by the open statement of the truth we would commend ourselves to everyone's conscience in the sight of God. . . . For God, who said, "Let light shine out of darkness," has shone in our hearts to give the light of the knowledge of the glory of God in the face of Jesus Christ. (2 Cor. 4:1–6)

Paul could preach the biblical history, the biblical story, and the biblical gospel of sin and salvation precisely because the

Bible's teaching of creation is true! Notice that, in commending God's Word, Paul goes back to the historicity of Genesis 1: "God, who said, 'Let light shine out of darkness.'" God made the entire universe and ordered it by the sheer power of his word. The Genesis creation account is true! For that reason alone, we may preach the Bible's teaching on Adam, man, sin, death, atonement, resurrection, and eternal life in a new heavens and new earth where there will be no death. God shone his light into the darkness of the dawn of creation, and when God's people humbly, simply, and faithfully hold fast the word of truth before the consciences of men, God's light shines into the darkness of the unbelieving heart with the light of the glory of God in the face of Jesus Christ.

We must not, therefore, abandon creation in the hopes of retaining some shred of the Christian doctrine of salvation. Moreover, we need not do so in order for Christianity to survive in a world dominated by darkness. How will Christianity go forward, and how will the church prevail through history? The book of Revelation answers: "They have conquered . . . by the blood of the Lamb and by the word of their testimony, for they loved not their lives even unto death" (Rev. 12:11).

6

God's Design for Gender, Marriage, and Sex

RICHARD D. PHILLIPS

Let marriage be held in honor among all, and let the marriage bed be undefiled, for God will judge the sexually immoral and adulterous. (Hebrews 13:4)

IN HIS PENETRATING BOOK, *One or Two: Seeing a World of Difference*, Peter Jones points out the similarities between the debaucheries of ancient Rome and the secular culture that Christians face in America and the West in the twenty-first century. According to Jones, "Rome was sports- and entertainment-mad, and choking on sexual excess."[1] The emperor

1. Peter R. Jones, *One or Two: Seeing a World of Difference* (Escondido, CA: Main Entry, 2010), 21. I would urge readers to read Jones's salient and important critique of the contemporary pagan assault on Christianity. Far from facing a true secularism, Christians today should realize that our culture is being recast by a

Nero embodied this decadent spirit, exulting in "prostitution orgies, homosexual and hermaphrodite trysts, gay marriage and pedophilia."[2] The apostle Paul was living in Rome during these years, and he wrote strong denunciations of sexual perversion from his prison cell in Nero's Rome (Eph. 5:4–6). It was also during these years that the savage persecution of Christians began in Rome, including the execution of both Peter and Paul. Followers of Jesus were described as "haters of humanity" because of their firm stand against pagan immorality,[3] just as Christians in America and the West are now accused of "hate crimes" for refusing to endorse sexual uncleanness and homosexual marriage.

In an environment like this, it is vital for Christians to know the difference between biblically prudent accommodations to culture and issues on which we cannot faithfully compromise. Two areas in which this question is raised relate to gender and sexuality. For a generation, the evangelical commitment to biblical marriage has included a complementarian view of men and women in relationship. Whereas the culture increasingly demands absolute egalitarianism, Christians have argued for the difference between men and women and their respective, complementary roles in marriage. In recent years, however, progressively minded evangelicals have sought to soften this area of conflict with a post-Christian culture. More and more evangelical churches are ordaining women to the biblical offices of elder and deacon or otherwise softening the restrictions on women in church leadership. While evangelicals have not abandoned a biblical view of marriage and sex, increasing voices are suggesting

radical mysticism that seeks to recover the ancient pagan vision of life. In addition to *One or Two*, I would recommend Jones's books *Gospel Truth, Pagan Lies* (Escondido, CA: Main Entry, 2012) and *Capturing the Pagan Mind* (Nashville: B&H, 2003).

2. Jones, *One or Two*, 21.
3. Tacitus, quoted in Jones, *One or Two*, 21.

a downplaying of complementarianism as well as the traditional Christian opposition to homosexual relations.

The purpose of this chapter is to explore some of the categories in which the Bible speaks with clarity on the subject of gender, marriage, and sexuality. In addition to providing biblical answers to questions about current topics of interest, I want to outline the resources, challenges, and blessings that God intends for his people in marriage and sex.

Mankind Created as Male and Female

When asking questions about human nature or society, the place to start is the opening chapters of the Bible, where God's creation design is set forth. We find clear distinctions made with respect to gender in the very creation of our race. In Genesis 1:26–27, where man's creation is introduced, we find three points emphasized. First, man was created to bear the image of God: "Then God said, 'Let us make man in our image, after our likeness'" (Gen. 1:26). This statement elevates the significance of man's created nature, since it indicates that God's purpose was to reveal himself by the creation of our race. Second, man's dominion over all other creatures is emphasized: "And let them have dominion over the fish of the sea and over the birds of the heavens and over the livestock and over all the earth and over every creeping thing that creeps on the earth" (Gen. 1:26). This statement contradicts the idea that man is just another animal, however highly developed. In contrast, the Bible says that man was made to mediate between God and the creatures, performing God's will on earth for the display of his glory. Third, the creation of mankind stresses the two genders in which mankind fulfills its calling: "So God created man in his own image, in the image of God he created him; male and female he created them" (Gen. 1:27). According to this foundational biblical teaching, man's calling both to bear God's image and to govern according to God's will requires the gender distinction inherent to our making.

Already we have enough information to begin forming a biblical approach to gender. Here we see both the fundamental unity of men and women in our human nature and also the clear distinction between the genders. Notice that gender—male and female—does not appear in the Bible as a social invention or construction, as is claimed by radical secularists today. Just as God created the human race, so God also made some humans into males and others into females. This picture is confirmed in Genesis 2:22, where we read that God took a rib from the man and fashioned it "into a woman and brought her to the man." The gender distinction within creation results from a definite and intentional act of God.

At the most basic level of every person's identity, therefore, in addition to our awareness of God and our shared humanity, is gender. We are all either *he* or *she*. We must all self-identify as either *himself* or *herself*—never merely as *self*. This distinction is grounded not in our self-assessment but in our biological and physiological makeup. We did not make ourselves male or female any more than we made ourselves human beings.

Christians today live in an age of rebellion against God that seeks to strike at the very foundations of how God created human identity and society. Our neo-pagan world pursues an agenda in which all distinctions among creatures are destroyed and merged into oneness. According to progressive cultural revolutionaries, there is no longer a distinction between the Creator and the creation, between life and death, between truth and error, between children and parents, or between male and female.[4] Seeing this strategy is a help to Christians who seek to gauge the significance of our resistance to cultural demands. Should we downplay gender distinctions in the church so as to avoid offending non-Christians? Without doubt, many Christians who suggest this strategy seek only to remove a potential barrier to their witness of the gospel of God's grace in Christ. The problem is that by accommodating themselves to such a pagan agenda, Christians fail in their most basic calling—to bear the image of God so as to reveal his truth and glory. Instead of conforming to secular demands that involve rebellion against God as Creator, Christians must confront the pagan vision of life with a Christian witness to biblical truth. When it comes to gender, this means that instead of downplaying the difference between men and women, Christians are to present the biblical vision of human life, in which men and women are united but categorically different.

In particular, Christians should resist the impulse toward androgyny, that is, the combination of male and female, that is presently so strong in Western society. Postmodern society would have men and women dress the same, groom themselves in the same way, take up the same roles in society and the home, and speak and act in the same ways. The media bombards our children with images of men in feminine roles, dress, and mannerisms and women in masculine roles, dress, and mannerisms—not to mention the agenda to impose homosexual norms and values. In response, Christian women should cultivate wholesome, natural, and godly femininity, and Christian men

---

4. It is this situation that provides Peter Jones with his title *One or Two*, the point of which is that paganism attacks God's creation authority by collapsing distinctions, whereas Christians are called to maintain the creation order and its God-designed distinctions.

should cultivate wholesome, natural, and godly masculinity. We must do this for God's sake, combating today's cultural rebellion against his creation design. And we must do so for the world's sake, bearing a living witness that reflects the truth, beauty, and blessing of God's creation design.

I have little doubt that many Christian women who read the above paragraph will recoil in hostility against a calling to cultivate a distinctively feminine life. No doubt many Christian men will likewise object. In doing so, however, they attest to the degree to which evangelical Christians today conform to unbiblical cultural norms rather than to clearly biblical lifestyles. Of course, it is true that women can be mistreated and taken advantage of when they embrace a biblical outlook on their lives. It was for this reason that Peter not only urged women to imitate Sarah in her submission to Abraham, but added that in this way they "do what is right" and "do not give way to fear" (1 Peter 3:6 NIV). Many of the fears that women experience result from male sins they have experienced, but other fears come from expectations and attitudes that have been imposed upon women by the feminism of an anti-Christian culture. Who decided that a full and rich life for women is gained mainly by imitating male roles and behaviors? According to the Bible's picture, a feminine role does not bar Christian women from exercising the full range of the gifts and talents God has given them—just consider the virtuous woman of Proverbs 31, who is anything but pigeonholed in a narrow life. The Bible does, however, call women to lead lives that are different from men in important respects. Likewise, many Christians have experiences that understandably cause them to fear manmade codes for dress and conduct that lack biblical warrant. Yet, as Paul makes clear in 1 Corinthians 11:1–15, there are masculine and feminine norms for dress, grooming, and behavior, and Christians honor

God by looking, talking, and acting according to the gender in which he sovereignly made us.

God created mankind to bear his image—the most essential point of which is that we are by our very natures, together with our actions, to bear testimony to God in the world. For this calling, the Bible says that "male and female he created them" (Gen. 1:27). The bearing of God's image requires distinct masculinity and distinct femininity, as well as the male-female love relationship that testifies to the love inherent to the triune God (1 John 4:8). Gender clarity and biblical gender relations are therefore essential, not only to a healthy human identity, but also to the Christian witness to our Creator God.

Marriage Designed for Complementary Ministry

Amid the hue and cry in demanding marriage rights for homosexuals, secular Western culture assumes that it is qualified to shape and define the building blocks of human society. In doing this, twenty-first-century man declares his right to act as God. The Bible counters this in Genesis 2 by asserting that God is the designer of human society, just as he was the Creator of humanity itself. In particular, Genesis 2 depicts marriage as an institution created and designed by God for his own glory and mankind's good.

As the Bible defines it, marriage is a lifelong covenant bond between a man and a woman. It is not by chance that the making of the first woman—both one with the first man, but also fashioned to be different from him—is bound up in the first marriage (Gen. 2:18–24). Genesis 2 concludes with a summation of what marriage is: "Therefore a man shall leave his father and his mother and hold fast to his wife, and they shall become one flesh" (Gen. 2:24). Jesus Christ confirmed this definition, pointing out that God "made them male and female," so that a marriage is established when a man leaves his father and mother and takes his wife, with the result that "the two shall become one flesh" (Matt. 19:4–5). According to Jesus, marriage assumes and requires the gender distinction with which God created humanity and the emotional/sexual combining that is possible only in heterosexual union.

As Genesis 2 describes it, marriage is designed by God for intimate, complementary, and mutual ministry between a man and a woman. Because of its intimacy, both sexually and emotionally, marriage is intended to be a lifelong commitment. Jesus taught, "So they are no longer two but one flesh. What therefore God has joined together, let not man separate" (Matt. 19:6; see also 1 Cor. 7:39). While it is certainly true that God designed marriage for the procreation of children, the more basic purpose of marriage is companionship and ministry. Marriage is thus introduced in Genesis 2:18 in this way: "Then the LORD God said, 'It is not good that the man should be alone; I will make him a helper fit for him.'" Man's aloneness is "the problem" for which marriage is "the answer," although it is clear from Genesis 1 that this was always God's intention and design. For the wife to be designated "a helper fit for him" is hardly a put-down, as feminism would make it out to be today. Women were made by God to relate to men, just as God made men dependent on their relationship with women (see 1 Cor. 11:11).

It is not by chance that Paul's teaching in Colossians 3:12–14, which has a general application to all Christian relationships, is so often cited with respect to marriage, just as it is followed by Paul's instructions for husbands and wives (Col. 3:18–19). Here the Bible sets a paradigm of grace received from God and extended to one another. Biblical marriage calls not for manipulation, but for mutual ministry through humble, forbearing, and forgiving love. In this respect, husbands and wives relate to another according to the same playbook and formula.

> Put on then, as God's chosen ones, holy and beloved, compassionate hearts, kindness, humility, meekness, and patience, bearing with one another and, if one has a complaint against another, forgiving each other; as the Lord has forgiven you, so you also must forgive. And above all these put on love, which binds everything together in perfect harmony. (Col. 3:12–14)

At the same time, the difference between men and women is reflected in different mandates for their relationship. Paul continues in Colossians to say,

> Wives, submit to your husbands, as is fitting in the Lord. Husbands, love your wives, and do not be harsh with them. (Col. 3:18–19)

As these mandates are expanded elsewhere in the New Testament, we can say that husbands are called to minister to their wives through loving encouragement and sacrificial service (Eph. 5:25–30; 1 Peter 3:7), and wives are called to minister to their husbands through helpful support and a respectful demeanor (Eph. 5:22–24, 33; 1 Peter 3:1–6). Mutual ministry, following the divine pattern for husbands and wives, makes marriage a blessed foundation for all human society and the context in which God's love and truth may reign in the believing home.

The biblical mandate for mutual ministry in marriage reveals some of God's purposes for mankind. It is clear that God intends for his people, male and female, to spend their lives learning to love. With this in mind, we can see in the garden a truth that is experienced in every marriage, namely, that love between men and women is difficult and costly. This was true even before the entry of sin, as seen in Genesis 2:18, "I will make him a helper fit for him." The word for "fit for him" (Hebrew, *kenegdo*) means "corresponding to him as an opposite number." Included is the idea that women, while suited for men, are also different from men. After all, when God took Adam's rib, he fashioned it into something of the same substance but of somewhat different design. Because husbands and wives are different, marital love requires effort, communication, and growth—the very things that God would have us spend our lives learning to do.

On top of this challenge, the problem of sin is added in Genesis 3. It is significant to note how the curses on the woman and the man affect their relationship. To the woman, God said, "I will surely multiply your pain in childbearing; in pain you shall bring forth children. Your desire shall be for your husband, and he shall rule over you" (Gen. 3:16). The first part of that curse refers to the pains involved with the entire reproductive process. Most significant to our study is the second half, which promises a sinful desire for women to contest the leadership of their marriage and the resulting conflict. We can see similar effects in God's curse on the man: "Cursed is the ground because of you; in pain you shall eat of it all the days of your life. . . . By the sweat of your face you shall eat bread, till you return to the ground" (Gen. 3:17–19). Here is the man, created to be a nurturing and protective lord of the garden (Gen. 2:15), now made its slave, with a sin-induced tendency to be too preoccupied with work to devote his attention to the needs of his wife.

Why is marriage so hard? The answer is twofold: because God wants us to learn how to love, by applying ourselves to this endeavor, and because sin has corrupted us, so that we need to repent and be restored to one another and to God through Jesus Christ. However difficult the marriage relationship may seem, it remains, when pursued through faith in the Lord, enormously blessed by God and the chief context in which God intends for earthly harmony to reign in our lives. Christians must therefore not only protect the definition of marriage, but also foster the blessing of marriage as male and female sinners come together in true love, empowered by the grace of God as it is received in Jesus Christ.

Marriage Designed as Romantic and Sexual

In emphasizing the companionship dynamics of marriage, it is possible for Christians, especially when overreacting to worldly sensuality, to downplay the romantic and sexual aspects of marital union. Christians sometimes hear that modern notions of romance are the creation almost *ex nihilo* of nineteenth-century French romantic novels. But anyone who has read the Song of Solomon, not to mention the book of Genesis, can rebut this claim easily. As God designed marriage, it has always involved romantic love and sexual delight. For this reason, Christians who downplay the calling for romance and sexuality in marriage fall short of the biblical ideal.

Consider the compelling story of Jacob and Rachel, which begins in Genesis 29. When Jacob arrived in the land of his uncle Laban, he noticed his two daughters. We are told that the difference between them lay in the realm of how attractive they were to him: "Leah's eyes were weak, but Rachel was beautiful in form and appearance" (Gen. 29:17). The point is not to endorse a merely outward orientation to attraction, but simply to note that sexual attraction is seen in the Bible as part of a married relationship. We are not surprised, therefore, to read, "Jacob loved Rachel" (Gen. 29:18). Because of his amorous affection for this younger sister, Jacob agreed to work for seven years, which "seemed to him but a few days because of the love he had for her" (Gen. 29:20). God has designed a strong romantic desire to motivate both men and women to fulfill their God-given ideal.

The sexual aspect of Christian marriage is highlighted in the Song of Solomon. In chapter 4, the male lover begins, "Behold, you are beautiful, my love, behold, you are beautiful!" (Song 4:1), and then proceeds to work his way down her body with sexually provocative imagery. When he says at the chapter's end, "Awake, O north wind, and come, O south wind! Blow upon my garden, let its spices flow" (Song 4:16), it is not agriculture that he has in mind.

This biblical portrait of sex needs to be emphasized among some Christians who suggest that marital love need not include a strong sexual attachment. This idea is simply wrong. While godly modesty should certainly be cultivated among young men and women, parents and churches do grave harm if they suggest that there is something dirty or repulsive about the opposite anatomy or the physical acts of sex.

The Song of Solomon does not, however, promote a licentious view of sexuality. Note that the sexual intimacy of this book takes place within the walls of a protected garden, after the locked door has been opened by the proper key (Song 4:12). While the Bible promotes God's design for romantic male-female attraction and intense sexual pleasure, these are intended only for the safeguarded relationship that is biblical marriage alone. Both a positive endorsement and a negative prohibition are therefore found in Hebrews 13:4, "Let marriage be held in honor among all, and let the marriage bed be undefiled." Christians must not treat married sexual intimacy as unclean in any way, but must preserve sexual intimacy only for the God-designed relationship of marriage, "for God will judge the sexually immoral and adulterous."

The Bible's numerous and strong injunctions against the sinful misuse of sexuality are worthy of careful note. Paul summarizes the entire Bible when he warns: "Do not be deceived: neither the sexually immoral, nor idolaters, nor adulterers . . . will inherit the kingdom of God" (1 Cor. 6:9–10). Sexual sin is antithetical to godly living, and therefore Christians are actively to avoid sexual temptation and proactively to cultivate a pure and chaste heart. This practice starts with the biblical injunction to "flee" from sexual temptation (1 Cor. 6:18; 2 Tim. 2:22). Like Joseph racing from the clutches of Potiphar's wife (Gen. 39:12), Christian men and women are aggressively to avoid sources of sexual temptation. This will include close relationships with the opposite sex, often in the workplace, that may lead to adultery. This will include a proactive policy against Internet pornography. Christians must realize the power of sexual attraction and the necessity of sexual purity, and take up an appropriate stance that will foster obedience and purity. This is where a healthy, biblical respect for the power of sexual allure informs wisdom among believers. Christians who wish to avoid sexual sin will simply avoid occasions for sexual temptation. This is vitally important for Christians who are dating or engaged but not yet married. Their attraction *should* be so strong that they are likely to weaken when faced with the combination of temptation and opportunity. With this in mind, those two are to be kept carefully apart. Christians who wish to avoid sexual sin will guard against its possibility in practical ways.

A biblically informed view of sexuality is bound to promote a high regard for marriage and encourage people with sexual desires to pursue marriage, which is precisely what God intends. In marriage, sex is an important part of the mutual ministry between a husband and wife. Paul frankly acknowledges the sexual needs of most people and the way that God designed sex to bind a couple emotionally.

> Because of the temptation to sexual immorality, each man should have his own wife and each woman her own husband. The husband should give to his wife her conjugal rights, and likewise the wife to her husband. (1 Cor. 7:2–3)

Notice the emphasis on giving rather than self-gratification: God designed sexual intimacy to be a ministry of a man and woman to one another. Paul goes so far as to say, "The wife does not have authority over her own body, but the husband does. Likewise the husband does not have authority over his own body, but the wife does" (1 Cor. 7:4). This statement does not, of course, give either partner the right to demand actions that are degrading or otherwise offensive. Paul's idea is simply to emphasize the right and obligation of ministry by means of the sexual acts of the body. For instance, a wife should realize the stress experienced by her husband in the world and should seek for the marriage bed to be a place of delight and refreshment. The husband should understand the wife's desire for attention and affirmation, and should make love to her in a way that ministers to these needs rather than ignores them. "Do not deprive one another," Paul adds, noting the significance of sexuality to the human makeup, "except perhaps by agreement for a limited time" (1 Cor. 7:5). Clearly, sexual ministry is an integral and vital aspect of mutual ministry in marriage.

God Abominates Sexual Perversion

When we see how important sexuality is to human life and relationships, and especially when we see how the Bible speaks of marital love as mirroring the believer's relationship to Jesus Christ (Eph. 5:32), we are not surprised at the Bible's severe language in condemning unnatural perversions of sex. These condemnations include the Bible's prohibition against sex between close family members. In 1 Corinthians 5:1, Paul is apoplectic at the news that a purportedly Christian man is having sex with his father's wife (evidently not his mother), noting that this is so contrary to nature that even pagans will not permit it. Likewise, Leviticus 18:6–18 uses the strongest language to abominate incest of any kind. Leviticus 20:10–21 provides a catalog of condemned sexual perversions, starting with adultery, moving through incest, adding homosexuality, and concluding with sex acts performed with animals.

In today's Western society, the subject of homosexuality warrants the most careful consideration under this heading of sexual perversion. We have already pointed out that God created us to bear his image within clearly defined genders (Gen. 1:26–27) and that the first woman was created within the context of God's provision for heterosexual marriage (Gen. 2:18–22). If the Bible is to be granted any relevant authority, then its extremely strong language in condemning homosexual sin must be taken as representing God's will.

One of the strongest condemnations of homosexuality is found in the opening section of Paul's gospel presentation in the book of Romans. Paul begins by declaring God's wrath against all who fail to respond to God's self-revelation in nature by worshiping him with thanks (Rom. 1:21). Having turned from God, unbelieving man unavoidably turns to idols. God, in judgment, "gave them up to dishonorable passions" (Rom. 1:25–26). Paul goes on to specify that he is referring to homosexual relations:

> For their women exchanged natural relations for those that are contrary to nature; and the men likewise gave up natural

relations with women and were consumed with passion for one another. (Rom. 1:26–27)

This language indicates that homosexual sin is more perverse than other forms of sexual license since it is "contrary to nature." In other words, in addition to violating God's written Word, homosexuality perverts the obvious order revealed in nature, committing an extreme offense to God. In this respect, Paul's language mirrors the revulsion seen in Old Testament passages like Leviticus 18:22: "You shall not lie with a male as with a woman; it is an abomination." Paul continues in this vein, condemning men who commit "shameless acts with men" and receive "in themselves the due penalty for their error" (Rom. 1:27). Paul thus teaches that homosexuality is itself a fitting punishment for a society that knowingly turns from God. The Bible's abomination of these sins is reflected in the intensity of Paul's descriptions: "impurity," "dishonoring of their bodies," "dishonorable passions," "contrary to nature," "shameless acts," and "a debased mind" (Rom. 1:24–28).

Unless the Bible's authority on this matter is overthrown by some ingenious hermeneutical tactic, the severe attitude of God is revealed by the intensity of Scripture's condemnation of this sin. This is not to say that homosexuals are more guilty before God because of this sin than, say, those who commit heterosexual adultery, since all sin brings each of us under God's infinite wrath. Nonetheless, the Bible does display a special distaste for the perversion of homosexual sin. Romans 1:21–28 stands out not as an exception to the Bible's general teaching but as a summary of it in the severe condemnation of homosexuality, calling for repentance and abstention from such acts (see also Lev. 20:13; 1 Cor. 6:9; 1 Tim. 1:10).

What about the claim, frequently heard today, that homosexuals were "made this way" by God, the point of which is often to morally neutralize this sin? First, God's attitude toward behavior is determined not by man's sinful state, but by his holy character as revealed in the Scriptures. Given the Bible's teaching against homosexuality, God's approval cannot be inferred from human desires, however widespread. Moreover, it is not surprising that, after the fall of our race into sin, men and women would have sinful desires and perhaps even be born with such inclinations. This does not justify sin, but condemns sinners for their perversity before God's holiness. Indeed, this problem is true of all of us in one way or another. Homosexuality is far from standing alone as a sinful inclination that condemns people before God. Rather, it is merely one of a legion of corruptions that mark us all as "fall[ing] short of the glory of God" (Rom. 3:23). In this respect, it is proper and necessary to emphasize that homosexuality is not a sin that uniquely condemns people before God. However strong the Bible's condemnations may be of this sin, and while this sin involves a particularly grievous violation of God's creation order, it remains just one of many sins by which our entire race is justly abhorred by God's holy justice. This being emphasized, the reality that a person may have lifelong desires does not justify them when they run contrary to God's Word.

A further concern is raised about people who admit to homosexual desires, but who realize the Bible's teaching against it and thus remain chaste. So far as their behavior goes, such people honor God by their faithful stance against temptation. It cannot be admitted, however, that their desire is morally neutral or acceptable to God so long as it is not indulged. Much of Paul's condemning language deals not merely with homosexual acts, but also with the perversity of the desire itself: "lusts of . . . impurity," "dishonorable passions," and "a debased mind" (Rom. 1:24–28). In this respect, homosexual desire is no different from any other sinful desire. In the Sermon on the Mount,

Jesus identified the desire to sin with the sinful act, pointing out that both violate God's law.

> You have heard that it was said to those of old, "You shall not murder; and whoever murders will be liable to judgment." But I say to you that everyone who is angry with his brother will be liable to judgment. (Matt. 5:21–22)

> You have heard that it was said, "You shall not commit adultery." But I say to you that everyone who looks at a woman with lustful intent has already committed adultery with her in his heart. (Matt. 5:27–28)

No Christian would argue that we should content ourselves with hearts filled with malice or sinful lust, but would point out the need for a renewed heart that is freed from these desires. The same must be maintained for homosexual drives, which through prayer and Scripture should be mortified by God's grace.

God Glorifies His Grace in Biblical Marriage and Sex

When we consider sexual sin of any kind, whether heterosexual or homosexual, the Bible's condemnation is clear. Paul writes: "Do you not know that the unrighteous will not inherit the kingdom of God? Do not be deceived: neither the sexually immoral, nor idolaters, nor adulterers, nor men who practice homosexuality . . . will inherit the kingdom of God" (1 Cor. 6:9–10). Given the full biblical definition of the seventh commandment in Matthew 5:27–28, there are none who could be justified by this standard. Thankfully, Paul continues with words that reflect Christ's saving mercy: "And such were some of you. But you were washed, you were sanctified, you were justified in the name of the Lord Jesus Christ and by the Spirit of our God" (1 Cor. 6:11).

What good news is here revealed! Such *were* you! In other words, Christians are no longer bound in such sin. Paul's description comprehends the grace of both justification and sanctification, the forgiveness of our sin and our moral transformation. There is saving grace for all who turn from sin to the cleansing grace of Christ! There is grace during our ongoing struggle, as Christ's blood advocates our forgiveness (1 John 2:1–2), and as God provides a way of escape (1 Cor. 10:13). There is grace after we sin, since God is "faithful and just to forgive us our sins and to cleanse us from all unrighteousness" (1 John 1:9). There is grace from Christ to conquer sin, as our hearts and minds are progressively renewed in the holiness of Christ (Eph. 4:23–24). Christ provides the conquering hope with which believers look forward to an ultimate victory against all sin: "Beholding the glory of the Lord, [we] are being transformed into the same image from one degree of glory to another" (2 Cor. 3:18).

God does not only glorify his saving grace in delivering us from sexual sin. He also glorifies his covenant love in faithful Christian marriage. As Paul teaches in Ephesians 5:33, a godly husband is able to "love his wife as himself" and a godly wife has grace to "see that she respects her husband." God glorifies his holiness in the sexual purity that he empowers among his people. In an age that simply assumes the inevitability of sexual indulgence, Christians are granted the Holy Spirit's power for "faithfulness" and "self-control," among other graces (Gal. 5:22–23). In the end, God will glorify his people who come in faith to Christ, putting on the white robe of righteousness that Jesus grants through faith and cultivates through his sanctifying grace. In the beginning, God created man and woman to bear his image in creation glory. At the end of redemption, God will present the entire company of the redeemed as the glorious bride to enjoy eternal bliss in the love of his Son. It is with this incomparable end in mind that Christians are wise to embrace now the biblical design for gender, marriage, and sex.

> And I saw the holy city, new Jerusalem, coming down out of heaven from God, prepared as a bride adorned for her husband. And I heard a loud voice from the throne saying, "Behold, the dwelling place of God is with man. He will dwell with them, and they will be his people, and God himself will be with them as their God." (Rev. 21:2–3)

7

Differing Views on the Days of Creation

DEREK W. H. THOMAS

IN APPROACHING the topic of the days of creation, we come to an issue that is somewhat complex and definitely divisive. Here Christians need grace to love one another, together with discernment in upholding Scripture. My approach will be to set forth the difficulties that are attached to any consideration of the creation days, as well as our understanding of the compatibility of Genesis 1 and Genesis 2. Before diving in, however, we need to reflect on the relationship between science and theology in general.

Relating Science and Theology

In relating the Bible and science, we must first appreciate that these represent worldviews regarding the nature of the universe.

The Big Bang theory, which teaches that the cosmos came into being as the result of a singularity, together with the theory of evolution, constitutes a worldview. It is a way of viewing the world as well as an epistemology—an understanding of how things are and how things are meant to be. It is one thing to address the scientific theory of evolution, but the fact of the matter is that evolution as a philosophy of life, as an epistemology, is what governs most of the people who believe that we have sprung from apes. The idea that we are the product of evolution, that man is on a continual course of evolving, is not merely a scientific theory but a philosophy. It is a way of life that affects ethics, morals, standards, and communities. This being the case, I think it is fair to ask about the relationship between science and theology, the relationship between science and the Bible.

This relationship is a matter about which Christians should be deeply concerned. We do not want to commit the church's error, in response to Galileo, of too readily assuming that the Bible teaches that the earth is at the center of the universe and that everything else is moving around it. There was a time when Christians believed that a literal reading of the Bible required the sun to move around the earth, since Joshua 10:13 states that "the sun stopped in the midst of heaven" at God's command to enable the Israelites to complete their victory over the five Canaanite kings. Upholding biblical authority, the church argued that the earth must be stationary while the sun moves around it. Galileo, among others, realized differently, observing that at least our solar system is heliocentric and not geocentric, and that the earth moves around the sun and not vice versa. For this teaching, Galileo was accused of heresy, convicted, and treated harshly by the church. Naturally, Christians do not want to commit that same error, just as we do not want to find ourselves out on a limb that has been sawn off. Wrongly interpreting the book of

Joshua, the church backed itself into a corner. Our desire not to repeat this mistake prompts reflection on the relationship between science and theology.

In response to this concern, we should note the difference between the Galileo controversy and the question of the original creation. When it comes to the days of creation and the origin of the universe, we have actually left the realm of science and entered the realm of philosophy and theology. The reason for this is that science in and of itself cannot answer the question, "From whence did we come?" The Big Bang theory does not answer this question because it only raises another question: "What was there before the singularity?" or "What caused the singularity?" To this question science offers few answers. Whatever it was that caused everything that we observe—whether it was ether or electromagnetism or something else—it has to be something eternal and sufficiently powerful to bring the entire universe into being. Whatever answer we give to creation becomes divine, since the attributes of deity are needed to bring the universe into being, and at this point science has moved outside its own sphere into the sphere of theology and philosophy.

Scientists get very antsy when theologians do science and, likewise, theologians should get antsy when scientists do theology. For if theologians do science badly, it is certainly true that scientists do theology badly. This relationship comes to bear on the issue of the age of the universe. According to current scientific thinking, the universe is nearly fourteen billion years old. Now, if you believe that the universe was created in six twenty-four-hour days, then how long has it been in existence? If you want to be generous, seeing gaps in the genealogies of Genesis, then you may get to 20,000 years. If you want to be very generous, you may get to 50,000 or even more years. But no matter how generous you are, if you take the Genesis text literally, you still come up with a number that is utterly incompatible with the findings of science. If you take the highest conceivable figure from the Bible—let's very generously say 200,000 years—and take the lowest number that science provides—let's say 4.5 billion years—the Bible and science remain utterly incompatible. The two views are universes apart, with no reconciliation possible. In order to reconcile the Bible with science, you have to do something radical to the Old Testament's account of creation and, with it, something radical to the origin of mankind.

In response to this situation, theologians and preachers can discard science entirely. This is not fair, of course, since we all trust science in many ways. When I go to visit a doctor and am told that I must have surgery, I am trusting my life to science. Of course, I am trusting my life to God when I go to the doctor, because I believe that God works through unbelievers as well as believers. But, in the context of that understanding, I am still trusting science. Similarly, I trust science when I get into an airplane or do many other things. So I must be careful not to discard science completely, lest I make myself look foolish.

When trying to determine the age of the universe, scientists observe that it looks very old. Light from the furthermost parts of the universe has reached us, and if you trust the science as to how large the universe is (and most conservative Christians do not have any quarrels at this point), then, based on its apparent rate of its expansion, it seems that the universe must indeed be very old. Given these calculations, arising from observations that scientists make, it simply is not possible to conclude that the universe was created only 50,000 years ago (or less). Based on observation, then, Christians may agree that God has created the universe with an apparent age that is much greater than that which Genesis 1 would indicate.

How, then, do young-earth creationists acknowledge the size of the universe and the speed of light, without agreeing to the old-age view of the scientists? One way is to challenge the principle of uniformitarianism as far as the speed of light is concerned. Theologian Douglas Kelly points to evidence that the speed of light may not be a constant, as scientists generally assume. He points out that the first careful measurement of the speed of light was taken in 1675. The figure produced then is 2.6 percent higher than today's figure. Some scientists have taken up this matter and noted an observable erosion of the speed of light over time. The point is that if the speed of light was greater at creation than it is now—studies suggest it was as much as seven million times faster—then light may have crossed the universe significantly faster than science assumes today. Kelly notes that at least one study of light using this paradigm would support a date around 4,400 BC, very much in line with a literal reading of Genesis.[1] I cite this as an example of creation theologians both presenting scientific theories and also showing the uncertain nature of the scientific enterprise.

Not all Christians are impressed by scientific theories like the one Kelly cites for the changing speed of light. But Christians are generally agreed in noting the shifts that take place in science. Science has moved from an Aristotelian view of astronomy to a Copernican view, and from a Newtonian to an Einsteinian view of physics, so science does change. In the early 1970s, I studied physics at university. What I was learning might as well have come from the eighteenth century, compared to views that are being advocated by physicists in university classes today. The point is that it is not only theologians who may be wrong, as were the Roman Catholic cardinals who persecuted Galileo for his teaching

---

1. Douglas F. Kelly, *Creation and Change: Genesis 1:1–2:4 in the Light of Changing Scientific Paradigms* (Ross-shire, UK: Christian Focus, 1997), 144–50.

about the solar system. Reformed theologians were once agreed that the pope is the Antichrist, but that view has been widely discarded by modern Reformed theologians. So theologians can be wrong. Science may also be wrong. We all have frames of references for our thinking, and while Christians maintain that the Bible is inerrant as God's Word, we all still import a universe of discourse into our reading of Scripture. This is our first step in relating science to theology: understanding that science and theology may both be wrong, but God's Word is not wrong.

Can Christians Accommodate Evolution?

Let's advance to relate science and theology specifically to the question of the origin of man. Here we must distinguish between Charles Darwin and the Darwinism of the twenty-first century, which is called neo-Darwinism. Neo-Darwinism is militantly atheistic, but Darwin was a deist. He believed that God originated the first simple life forms, that endless species evolved from them by natural laws of divine establishment. To be sure, Darwin's deism was no gospel, but his evolution was unlike that of neo-Darwinists that Christians are meeting today, especially in writings like Richard Dawkins's *The Selfish Gene*.

Richard Dawkins believes that there is no origin and no fixed point. He sees an unbroken line from mollusk to man. His is a reductionism in the absolute sense of that term, and this is the most dominant philosophy in modern thought, that everything is evolution and there are no limits or boundaries whatsoever. In this view, man is still evolving and may end up as virtually anything at all.

The Bible radically contradicts the philosophy of today's neo-Darwinism. This situation highlights the teaching of various

Christians today on the origin of Adam as the first man. Here we must differentiate between the so-called "historical Adam" and the biblical Adam. Many Christians today are insisting on belief in a historical Adam, not realizing that this is not necessarily the same as the biblical Adam. It is possible to believe that Adam really was a historical person, but that he was simply one whom God singled out from other hominids to bear his image in a special way. This would be a historical Adam, but, as one who arose from preexisting hominids, he would be very different from the Adam of the book of Genesis. Genesis 2:7 makes clear that Adam was created out of the dust of the ground. He was not formed by being corralled away from his fellow hominids. The biblical Adam was created by God's immediate action from the dust of the ground. It is hard to see that one is upholding an inerrant view of Scripture if Genesis 2:7 is made to say that God created Adam out of preexisting hominids rather than out of the literal dust of the ground.

One attempt to synthesize evolution with biblical creation is Denis Alexander's book *Creation or Evolution: Do We Have to Choose?*, which has been influential in recent years.[2] Alexander's thesis is that modern humans emerged 200,000 years ago, and that language developed 50,000 years ago. Somewhere between 6,000 and 8,000 years ago, God took a couple of Neolithic farmers and revealed himself to them in a special way. This divine revelation constituted Adam and Eve as *homo divinus*, bearing the image of God. Sadly, an embryonic form of this view was approved by John Stott in his book *Understanding the Bible*.[3] The view has been rebutted in recent years by Michael Reeves in *Should Christians Embrace Evolution?*[4]

2. Denis R. Alexander, *Creation or Evolution: Do We Have to Choose?* (Oxford: Monarch, 2008).

3. John R. W. Stott, *Understanding the Bible* (Grand Rapids: Zondervan, 1982).

4. Michael Reeves, "Adam and Eve," in *Should Christians Embrace Evolution?: Biblical and Scientific Responses*, ed. Norman C. Nevin (Phillipsburg, NJ: P&R, 2011), 43–56.

The key issue is whether or not Adam and Eve evolved from preexisting hominids from whom they were then separated. Did Adam and Eve come from lower forms? And were their evolutionary predecessors also in the image of God? Was the only difference for Adam and Eve that they, as *homo divinus*, understood what that meant, whereas their parents did not?

It should be clear that this line of reasoning involves a radical reinterpretation of Genesis 1:26–27, which says that Adam was made in the image of God. In Alexander's view, this simply means that they were in relationship with God. So what was the image of God before Adam and Eve, in the case of their parental hominids?

It should be obvious that any view that questions Adamic solidarity in creation will undermine other doctrines, such as that of original sin. Paul says that "death reigned through that one man," so that through faith we may "reign in life through the one man Jesus Christ" (Rom. 5:17). Paul's argument here presupposes, without any equivocation whatsoever, the existence of a historical, biblical Adam, and also that all of humankind descends from that one source, Adam and Eve. The entire argument in Romans 5 is linked, not merely to a historical Adam, but to Adam as the first human being. Without this biblical Adam, Romans 5 does not work.

It should be obvious as well that to deny the traditional view of Adam is to deny biblical inerrancy. This is the position taken by Peter Enns, who frankly declares that Paul was mistaken in his view of Adam. He says that Paul simply adopted a view that was current in his time.[5] Enns has been sliding down not only a slippery slope, but an alpine slope, away from biblical orthodoxy. Once the Bible's teaching can be dismissed as merely accommo-

---

5. Peter Enns, *The Evolution of Adam: What the Bible Does and Doesn't Say about Human Origins* (Grand Rapids: Brazos Press, 2012), 139.

dating to the cultural norms of the writers' times, the authority of Scripture has been completely lost. This same approach is taken to accommodate homosexuality, by dismissing biblical condemnations as merely reflecting primitive moral sensibilities. And once we can contradict culturally-offensive biblical teachings, like those condemning homosexuality or opposing evolution, why stop there? The notion of substitutionary atonement, through the shedding of Jesus' blood, as necessary to be forgiven, is not compatible with modern thinking, so why shouldn't we reject that biblical teaching, too?

This issue becomes important to the question of the age of the earth and the days of creation. Any view that questions a young human existence is simply not compatible with the doctrine of biblical inerrancy. Now, it is possible to accept an old earth and posit a more recent creation of Adam. But the genealogical record of humankind cannot be more than ten or twenty thousand years old and still adhere to the Bible. In fact, this is a generous allowance, since the Bible requires the human race to have begun no later than six to eight thousand years ago.

Some seek to address the question of evolution by appealing to theistic evolution. This view says that God created, but then withdrew himself in order to allow the natural process of evolution to take its course. An exception is sometimes made for God's ongoing involvement in the creation of the human soul or the human spirit. But did evolution stop at Adam? After all, if evolution is God's way of creating, then ten or fifty thousand years from now, we may have evolved into something other than human. In what sense, then, do we understand mankind to be made in the image of God? The point is that attempts to accommodate evolutionary theory inevitably end up compromising essential biblical doctrines, such as the doctrine that man bears the image of God.

Views of the Creation Days

Let's now turn to the creation accounts and the various theories regarding the age of the earth. Let me begin with the day-age view, which understands the days of creation as long days, perhaps millions of years, which would then account for the geological ages theorized by science.

An immediate question is whether or not the Hebrew word *yom*, for "day," can be used in this way. The answer is that *yom* is used in at least four different ways in Genesis 1 and 2. In Genesis 1:5, "day" means "daytime" as opposed to nighttime. There, "day" is twelve hours long. In the second half of that verse, "day" includes both daytime and nighttime, so it contains twenty-four hours in that case. In Genesis 2:1, "day" is equivalent to eternity, because it has not ended. In Hebrews 4:3–11, this Sabbath day is equivalent to eternity and not to twenty-four hours. Moving to Genesis 2:4, the day is indefinite, as when we say, "back in my day." Here we are referring to a general period in the past. So even in Genesis 1 and 2, there is variation as to the usage of *yom*. This shows that the argument cannot be solved merely on linguistic, semantic, or etymological understandings of the Hebrew word for day.

It is initially possible, then, that the day-age view is correct in seeing long creation days. Some of the days may have lasted millions of years, and others may have been much shorter. This is the view held by Hugh Ross and Gleason Archer in *The Genesis Debate*.[6] This view helps address the issue of light traveling across space without requiring that God created the universe with light already part way across the universe or that the speed of light was exponentially faster at the beginning than it is now.

---

6. David Hagopian, ed., *The Genesis Debate: Three Views on the Days of Creation* (Mission Viejo, CA: Crux Press, 2000).

According to the day-age view, millions of generations of life predate humans. The different species arose at different times in response to the changing environment, with many of them becoming extinct. This means that there was death before the fall among the plants and animals.

In my view, the cultural mandate in Genesis 1:28 was also a mandate for hunting, so that the issue of death before the fall is a nonissue, since even eating plants involved death. There is constant death within the vegetable world, so the simplistic question of death before the fall is not nuanced enough. The day-age view sees Romans 5:12 as pertaining to human death, not to death generally and the second law of thermodynamics, which they argue has operated from the beginning of creation.

Yet there are problems with the day-age view. First, it does not remove the controversy between science and the Bible, since science posits a different sequence of events than that found in Genesis 1. For example, the sun appears on day four in Genesis 1, after the sea, the land, and vegetation.

A variation on this theme is the gap theory. Here, instead of the days stretching for millions of years, there is a huge gap between Genesis 1:2 and Genesis 1:3, and perhaps between chapters 2 and 3. Yet the actual days of creation activity are restricted to twenty-four-hour days. "There was evening and there was morning, the first day" (Gen. 1:5), and "there was evening and there was morning, the second day" (Gen. 1:8), but in between them was a long gap. In this scheme, you have twenty-four-hour days adding up to one week, but can still allow for a genuinely old earth. This impression is heightened by English translations that use paragraph gaps between the days of creation. It then does not take much effort to imagine a gap between the verses—not merely on the page, but in history as well.

The gap theory was held by the Scofield Bible and by Donald Grey Barnhouse, as well as the beloved Scottish Presbyterian Thomas Chalmers. The idea is that when Genesis 1:2 says that "the earth was without form and void" (Hebrew, *tohu* and *bohu*), this reflects the rebellion among angels and the casting out of Satan from heaven. This view was once so prominent that Bernard Ramm stated in 1954,

> The Gap Theory has become the standard interpretation through hyper-orthodoxy, appearing in an endless stream of books, booklets, Bible studies, and periodical articles. In fact, it has become so sacrosanct with some that to question it is equivalent to tampering with Sacred Scripture or to manifest modernist leanings.[7]

The benefit of the gap theory is that it accommodates geological ages. It suggests that God destroyed the original creation because of Satan's influence on it, only to reshape it again. This, it is urged, would give some explanation for the geological ages that we see in the earth's makeup. Despite this benefit, the gap theory rests upon suppositions and has no actual biblical data to support it, especially since "without form and void" in Genesis 1:2 does not convey the idea of a cataclysmic devastation.

Another view is the analogical days view. It is similar to the gap theory in that Genesis 1:2 is understood as covering an indefinitely long period of time. Its most noteworthy advocate is C. John Collins of Covenant Theological Seminary. Collins asserts that *yom* in Genesis 1 refers to literal days, but speaks of them in an analogical way to represent God's creative activity. These days are not our week days, but God's work days. Given

7. Bernard Ramm, *The Christian View of Science and Scripture* (Grand Rapids: Eerdmans, 1954), 135.

this, the length of time actually involved in creation is irrelevant to the Bible's message.[8]

Yet another view is the literary framework view, which allows for long creation days, though this is not necessary to the view. This was first suggested by Johann Gottfried von Herder in the late eighteenth century. Today, the view is more likely to be associated with Meredith Kline. In Kline's scheme, Genesis 1 is a literary framework, and Genesis 2 is the normal account of history. As Kline sees it, Genesis 2:5 proves that Genesis 1 and 2 cannot both be treated as history: "When no bush of the field was yet in the land and no small plant of the field had yet sprung up—for the LORD God had not caused it to rain on the land, and there was no man to work the ground." There, Kline notes, we see normal providence at work, with vegetation growing up as rains water it, whereas in Genesis 1 we see something other than normal providence, since there the vegetation appears even before the creation of the sun. This cues us, Kline asserts, to see Genesis 1 as a literary, rather than a literal, account of creation.

The framework of this hypothesis is seen in the parallelism between the first three and the second three creation days. In the first three, light, sky, seas, dry land, and vegetation arise. In the second three days, there are lights in the heavens and living creatures teeming in the seas, in the sky, and on dry land. In this view, Genesis 1 is arranged not as a historical account but as a literary presentation of God's creation. The power of this account results from its attention to exegetical data. However, its critics point out that it misreads the genre of Genesis 1 as poetry rather than historical narrative. The framework hypothesis is held by a large number of conservative Reformed seminary professors, but vigorously rejected by its critics.

8. C. John Collins, *Science and Faith: Friends or Foes?* (Wheaton, IL: Crossway, 2003).

Still another view of the creation days is that God created the world in six twenty-four-hour days, but that he created it to look old. On this mature creation view, God created the geological strata, fossil remains, an expanding universe, and beams of light. This view harmonizes a literal reading of Genesis 1 with scientific data, but the main criticism of it is that God would not have created in a deceptive manner.

This argument about deception works both ways. When Adam opened his eyes and looked at Eve, she was a mature, adult woman, not a newborn. Was God deceiving Adam? Again, did Adam have a belly button? Did Eve? If they did, does this suggest deception on God's part, since it implies that they had come from a mother's womb?

The answer is that this is not deception. This is God creating things naturally, but mature. Perhaps it should be better thought of as testing: that if God makes the world look old, as though it sprang from a Big Bang, we are challenged to believe the scriptural teaching that the Bible originated by the word of almighty God. I would see this situation as testing, rather than deception, and God is certainly testing scientists in this regard every day, especially in the midst of an atheistic scientific community. In the same way that a fruit tree in the garden was not allowed to be eaten, God may be testing us with the scientific evidence of the universe.

Finally, we have the young earth view, in which God created the universe in six consecutive, twenty-four-hour days. This is the kind of straightforward reading of the text that we would expect for standard historical narrative. Genesis 1 does not have a warning at its top saying, "Do not read this chapter as though it were literal." This is the view, then, that is most natural when reading the text with no outside, contrary evidence.

The problem with this view is that we have evening and morning for the first three days, when there is no sun until day four. It is problematic to have a day when you do not have a sun, since a day is measured by the movement of the earth with respect to the sun. The answer is given that there must have been a non-solar light source for the first three days. The physics may demand a moon of some kind to perform this function. This is, of course, a bizarre idea within a non-theistic worldview, because creation veers off course with even a tiny amount of variance, rendering the emergence of life impossible. It is possible that the young earth view necessitates a different physics prior to the fall, which may account for the differing speeds of light over time. In any case, the literal view of creation days involves special, not normal, providence, as the matter of light on the fourth day proves.

According to the young earth view, the earth is around 10,000 years old, and fossilization is explained by catastrophism, that is to say, flood geology. This requires not just a local flood, but a worldwide flood to explain fossilization.

A survey of these views calls for me to make a selection. If I am forced to choose from all these creation views, I can certainly be comfortable with a young earth view that relies on catastrophe to explain the geological evidence, if the science of this theory holds true. I am more comfortable, however, with the mature creation view, in which God creates the universe to look old. My reason for favoring this view is that I doubt that the science of catastrophism will hold up in light of the fossil evidence and geological record. Both of these are literal, twenty-four-hour, six-day views of creation, and I prefer them because they involve the most straightforward reading of the text in accordance with its genre as historical narrative.

8

Christ, the Second Adam

JOEL R. BEEKE

*For as in Adam all die, even so in Christ shall
all be made alive. (1 Corinthians 15:22)*

WE LIVE IN AN AGE of individualism, a time when
many know how to say "I" and "me," but few understand the
significance of "we" and "us." Peter Lewis writes, "In this hyper-
individualistic age we, in the Western world anyway, like to
think of ourselves as self-contained units."[1] We drive to work in
separate cars and sit in our separate cubicles. We may feel more
connected to an Internet "friend" whom we have never met than
we do to our next-door neighbors.

It may seem strange to us that our lives should be bound up
with the life and actions of someone else. We tend to believe that

1. Peter Lewis, *The Glory of Christ* (London: Hodder and Stoughton, 1992), 203.

we are independent beings, each one crafting his own future or forging her own fate. It seems especially strange that our lives would be bound up in two figures in history, neither of whom has walked on the earth for thousands of years. The Bible, however, teaches us that the identity and destiny of all mankind depend either on Adam, the father of the human race, or on Jesus Christ, the incarnate Son of God.

In 1 Corinthians 15:47, Paul describes these two historical beings as "the first man," that is, Adam, and "the second man," Christ. Thomas Goodwin remarks that Paul speaks as if those two men were the only ones who ever lived, because they had the rest of humanity, as it were, hanging from their belts.[2] What a picture that is, Adam and Christ, standing like giants with millions, even billions, of people hanging upon them. The destiny of every man and woman who has ever lived hangs upon one of these two persons. Adam and Christ stand as the representatives of two eras, two worlds, and, we may say, two creations.[3]

The Holy Scriptures make it clear that we should look upon Adam as a figure or type of Christ, and look upon Christ as the second Adam. Romans 5:14 says that "Adam . . . is the figure of him that was to come." In 1 Corinthians 15:45, Paul calls Christ "the last Adam." Romans 5 and 1 Corinthians 15 make no sense unless we accept the fact that God deals with individuals in

2. Thomas Goodwin, *Christ Set Forth*, in *The Works of Thomas Goodwin* (1861; repr., Grand Rapids: Reformation Heritage Books, 2006), 4:31. On Adam and Christ, see Goodwin, *Of the Creatures*, in *Works*, 7:69–128.

3. "Adam and Christ here [in 1 Cor. 15:22] stand over against each other as the two great figures at the entrance of two worlds, two aeons, two 'creations,' the old and the new; and in their actions and fate lies the decision for all who belong to them, because these are comprehended in them and thus are reckoned either to death or to life. This is now expressed by 'in Adam' and 'in Christ'" (Herman Ridderbos, *Paul: An Outline of His Theology*, trans. John Richard de Witt [Grand Rapids: Eerdmans, 1975], 61).

solidarity with either Adam or Christ as their head.[4] When we consider the teaching of these two great chapters, together with the larger context of Scripture, we see that *Christ is the second Adam upon whom all our hope depends*. If we are not hanging upon Christ, then we are without God in the world, having no hope (Eph. 2:12).

Though few people today understand and appreciate Christ as the second Adam, this connection is a major doctrine in the Holy Scriptures. It is not touched upon lightly in a few verses here or there. It is a great river that flows through the Bible and waters many Scripture passages that do not even mention Adam.

The Work of the Second Adam

As the eternal Son of God, Christ was already alive with the Father at the first moment of creation. The gospel of John tells us, "In the beginning was the Word, and the Word was with God, and the Word was God," and this Word is the same person who became flesh, the only begotten Son of God (John 1:1, 14, 18; Ps. 33:6). By a special act of creation, the triune God made Adam's body out of the dust of the ground (Gen. 2:7) and breathed life into the first man by the Spirit (Job 33:4). How amazing it is to think that God the Son cooperated with his Father to create Adam (John 1:3), knowing that, as Christ, he would one day take the very same flesh-and-blood human nature to himself. Like Adam, Christ's human nature was formed by a special act of creation. He was made in the womb of a virgin

4. "This passage [Rom. 5:12–21] is eviscerated of its governing principle if these two solidaric relationships are not appreciated, and it is futile to try to interpret the passage except in these terms" (John Murray, *The Epistle to the Romans* [repr., Grand Rapids: Eerdmans, 1980], 179).

and of her substance alone, conceived not by the seed of man but by the supernatural power of the Holy Spirit (Matt. 1:20). Formed by the Holy Spirit, Christ was holy (Luke 1:35), set apart in moral purity and consecrated to the redemptive work of God.

In discussing Christ's work as the second Adam, I will address his calling and temptation, his obedience unto death, his gift of righteousness, and his resurrection to life.

The Second Adam's Calling and Temptation

As soon as he created the first Adam, the Lord God gave him a calling or task to fulfill. Genesis 2:15–17 tells us that he put Adam in the garden and commissioned him "to dress it and to keep it." God authorized him to eat of the variety of beautiful and delicious trees in the garden and gave him a law prohibiting him from eating from one tree as a test of his obedience. Adam was created to be a servant of the Lord. Genesis 2:15 literally says that God put man into the garden of Eden "to serve" it (Hebrew, *abad*, rendered "to dress" in the KJV).[5]

As God the Son, coequal, coessential, and coeternal with the Father and sharing the same divine nature (Phil. 2:6), he was not subject to the law, for he was the lawgiver. But he voluntarily placed himself under the law when he took our human nature to himself. He took "the form of a servant" (Phil. 2:7), one bound as a slave (Greek, *doulos*) to obey his Master. Galatians 4:4 says that "when the fulness of the time was come, God sent forth his Son, made of a woman, made under the law." In his incarnation, God's Son embraced the obligation to keep the moral law, which "God gave to Adam . . . by which He bound him and all his

5. The verb *abad* can be used of working the ground or other labor (Gen. 2:5; 3:23; 4:2, 12; Ex. 20:9), but it commonly refers to the labor of a servant or slave done in submission to authority (Gen. 14:4; 15:13–14; 25:23; 27:29, 40; 29:15, 18, 20; Ex. 6:5, etc.). It is also used for the service of worshiping God (Ex. 3:12; 20:5).

posterity to personal, entire, exact, and perpetual obedience" (Westminster Confession, 19.1, 5). In his particular coming as an Israelite, Christ also accepted the obligation to keep all the other ordinances the Lord had given to Israel (19.3, 4).

Christ also accepted the special command of God to serve as the mediator of the covenant of grace. He came as the Servant of the Lord, as foretold by Isaiah. God sent him to save both Jew and Gentile by pouring out his soul unto death and bearing the sins of many (Isa. 42:1; 49:3, 5, 6; 53:11). Isaiah 51:3 even says that the Lord's salvation will make the "wilderness like Eden" and the "desert like the garden of the LORD." God sent his servant as the second Adam to restore all that the first Adam had lost.

Luke 3 records that when the time came for Christ to begin his official ministry, and he was being baptized by John, the Holy Spirit descended upon Jesus in the visible form of a dove to anoint him with power from on high. God the Father announced from heaven, "Thou art my beloved Son; in thee I am well pleased" (Luke 3:22). In this account, we hear echoes of Isaiah 42:1, "Behold my servant, whom I uphold; mine elect, in whom my soul delighteth; I have put my spirit upon him: he shall bring forth judgment to the Gentiles." It is no accident that after the announcement that Christ is the Son of God, Luke traces out his human genealogy ultimately to "Adam, which was the son of God" (Luke 3:38). Christ is a new Adam, the head of a new posterity, and for their redemption he is anointed and empowered by the Holy Spirit to be the Servant of the Lord.

Adam had to face the challenge of the serpent's temptation, and so did the second Adam. After tracing the lineage of Christ back to Adam, the very next verses report that

Jesus being full of the Holy Ghost returned from Jordan, and was led by the Spirit into the wilderness, being forty days tempted of the devil. And in those days he did eat nothing: and when they were ended, he afterward hungered. (Luke 4:1–2)

Robert Peterson writes, "The result is an implied contrast between the two Adams and the testing they underwent."[6] How much more potent and complex was Christ's temptation! Adam was tempted in the fullness of his strength, placed in a beautiful garden, surrounded by all the luscious fruit that he could desire, restrained from eating from only one tree that the Lord God had forbidden to him. Christ was tempted in a barren wilderness, led by the Spirit to abstain from all food, and after forty days was weak, tired, and desperately hungry for the least morsel of bread. Adam faced but one temptation, but Christ on this occasion faced temptations on three distinct fronts. And whereas Adam fell, Christ stood firm against the Devil and put him to flight. Praise the Lord!

We should view Christ's facing temptation by the Devil in the same way that the Israelites saw David face the challenge of the giant Goliath. Behold our champion! If he falls, then all God's people fall. But Christ did not fall. He won the victory by obedience to the Word of God, three times repulsing Satan's temptations by invoking what God says in Scripture as a law that he had to keep. Christ afterward proceeded to cast out demons as a king who has routed the enemy's army (Luke 4:33–36, 41; 11:20). It is true that we can learn much from Christ about resisting temptation, but Christ is more than an example for us to follow. He is the new Adam, our champion who decisively defeated our enemy and blazed a trail of obedience that will bring many sons to glory. He has crushed the serpent under his feet and ours.

6. Robert A. Peterson, *Salvation Accomplished by the Son: The Work of Christ* (Wheaton, IL: Crossway, 2012), 469.

But after the wilderness temptation, Satan was not done with Christ (Luke 4:13), nor was Christ's work of "learning obedience" through suffering as yet complete (Heb. 5:8).

The Second Adam's Obedience unto Death

The incarnate Christ humbled himself and "became obedient unto death, even the death of the cross" (Phil. 2:8). This was the summit of Christ's work, and it consisted in obedience to the very end. As Christ comes to offer himself as a sacrifice for all sin, once and for all time, David hears him saying, "Lo, I come to do thy will, O God" (Ps. 40:6–8; Heb. 10:5–10).

In Romans 5, the apostle Paul compares Adam and Christ precisely by pointing out this matter of obedience—of doing the will of God. Romans 5:12 says, "By one man sin entered into the world." Verse 14 speaks of the transgression of Adam, "who is the figure of him that was to come." In other words, Adam prefigured Christ with respect to obedience or disobedience to the demands of the law of God.[7] In verse 15, we read of "the offence of one." Verse 16 says we fell "by one that sinned." And so it continues through verse 19, as Paul recalls "one man's disobedience." This is the history and legacy of the first Adam: sin, transgression, offense, and disobedience.

The second Adam stands in stark contrast to the first. Romans 5:18 speaks of "the righteousness of one."[8] Verse 19 declares the good news that "by the obedience of one shall many be made righteous." Christ's lifelong obedience reached its highest expression in his voluntary offering up of himself on the cross

7. Murray, *Romans*, 188.
8. It is also translated "one act of righteousness" (Rom. 5:18 ESV). In the Greek (*di' henos dikaiōmatos*), the grammar allows for "one" (*henos*) to be either an adjective modifying "righteousness" ("through one righteousness") or a masculine substantive in genitive relationship to "righteousness" ("through righteousness of one [man]").

for sinners (Phil. 2:8), which Paul celebrates in Philippians 2:6–11 and returns to again in Romans 6. Yet we must not lose sight of the fact that the work of the second Adam was not merely to die but to obey, and to obey in all things. His obedience must be imputed or accounted to us, or we cannot be accounted righteous before God. John Owen said, "Hereby many are made righteous. How? By the imputation of that obedience [of Christ] unto them. For so, and no otherwise, are men made sinners by the imputation of the disobedience of Adam."[9]

Jonathan Edwards wrote that Romans 5 "plainly shows that as what Adam did brought death, as it had the nature of disobedience, so what Christ did brought life, not only as a sacrifice, but as it had the nature of meriting obedience." This twofold obedience was necessary, Edwards explained, because "Christ's active obedience was as necessary to retrieve the honor of God's law and authority as his suffering."[10] God's law both demanded obedience and threatened death to the disobedient. Christ had to fulfill the law in both ways by perfectly obeying its precepts in life and by fully accepting and suffering its penalty in his death.

We must not separate Christ's obedience from his suffering and death. Christ's obedience was agonizing. The first man fell in a garden, and in the garden of Gethsemane we see another man fall to the ground in mortal agony of soul, crying out, "Abba, Father, all things are possible unto thee; take away this cup from me: nevertheless not what I will, but what thou wilt" (Mark 14:36). Here Christ spoke of the cup of God's wrath

---

9. John Owen, *The Doctrine of Justification by Faith*, in *The Works of John Owen* (repr.; Edinburgh: Banner of Truth, 1965), 5:334.

10. *The Works of Jonathan Edwards*, 14:398, quoted in Craig Biehl, *The Infinite Merit of Christ: The Glory of Christ's Obedience in the Theology of Jonathan Edwards* (Jackson, MS: Reformed Academic Press, 2009), 180, 134.

against sinners. Psalm 11:6 says, "Upon the wicked he shall rain snares, fire and brimstone, and an horrible tempest: this shall be the portion of their cup" (see also Ps. 75:8). It is a cup seething with the fire of a thousand volcanoes. In Isaiah 51:22, the Lord calls it "the cup of my fury."[11] The first Adam sinned by putting in his mouth an enticing piece of fruit. Christ took a cup full of bitter hellfire, cried out, "Thy will be done," and drank it to the dregs for us when he died upon the cross. If we belong to Christ, we will never have to drink from that bitter cup. We drink from another cup, the cup of salvation (Ps. 116:13), for he himself has become the portion of our cup (Ps. 16:5).

The Second Adam's Gift of Righteousness

The glorious obedience of the second Adam is our righteousness and the ground of our justification from all transgressions of the law. Just as Adam's disobedience brought woe, sickness, and death, so Christ's obedience brings joy, healing, and eternal life. Adam's sin brought abundant condemnation and death, but now justification and life abound much more through Christ's obedience. We see that in Romans 5:18: "Therefore as by the offence of one judgment came upon all men to condemnation; even so by the righteousness of one the free gift came upon all men unto justification of life."

Paul explains that the action of "one" overflows and accrues to the benefit of "many" (Rom. 5:15, 19). He even says that the disobedience or obedience of "one" led to the condemnation or justification of "all men" (Rom. 5:18). Paul writes in 1 Corinthians 15:22, "As in Adam all die, even so in Christ shall all be made alive." Paul did not write, "*because of* Adam all die," or "*like* Adam all die," but "*in* Adam all die." So also, Paul says, "*in*

11. See also Ps. 75:8; Jer. 25:15, 17, 28; Ezek. 23:31–33; Rev. 14:10; 16:19.

Christ shall all be made alive." Paul uses the phrase "in Christ" or "in him" countless times to signify our union with Christ as members of the body of which he is the head. This is not false mysticism, but the biblical, covenantal idea that one man can act as the representative of many.[12]

It is as if there were two great circles. At the center of one circle is the first Adam, and at the center of the second circle is Christ, the second Adam. Everyone inside the circle is connected to the person at the center. Paul is not saying that every single person will be made alive because of Christ. Rather, he is teaching that all who are united to Christ share in both his righteousness and his life. What one man did affects all who are in him, whether the man is Adam or Christ.

What kind of a connection is this? Certainly it is a union that has spiritual implications. Adam's disobedience brings both physical and spiritual death to all those born of him by natural generation. Christ's obedience saves body and soul—all those united to him by a Spirit-worked faith. Yet this connection has a foundation deeper than and prior to our faith, because Christ represented his people before they trusted in him—indeed, before they were born. It is a union based on the bond of a covenant—a legal bond formed by God's promise. As covenant heads and representatives, Adam and Christ brought either condemnation or justification to their people. Condemnation and justification are legal words pertaining to a person's standing in a court of law. This implies that God made a legal arrangement with both Adam and Christ so that the actions of each had consequences for their offspring, either physical (Adam) or spiritual (Christ).

12. Ridderbos, *Paul*, 38, 62. It has been called "corporate personality" or "corporate solidarity" and finds faint echoes in other leaders or fathers in the Old Testament who represented their people.

Christ's work has meaning only in the context of the covenant of grace.[13] We saw from Isaiah that God made promises to Christ as his servant. God promised that Christ himself would be a covenant for the people (Isa. 42:6; 49:8). God announced these promises centuries before Jesus was born. In fact, in Titus 1:2 Paul writes of the "hope of eternal life, which God, that cannot lie, promised before the world began." Before we knew Christ, before we were born, before Christ was born as the incarnate Son of God—in fact, before the dawn of creation—God established a covenantal relationship between his Son and his people. Christ spoke of this bond when he said that the Father had given people to him to save (John 6:39; 10:29; 17:2, 6, 12, 24). It is true that we are not "in Christ" in a vital and life-giving way unless and until we are united to him by the Spirit and by true faith (Rom. 16:7; 2 Cor. 13:5). But in the covenanted purposes of God, we were in Christ before time began (Eph. 1:3–4).[14] The Westminster Larger Catechism (Q. 31) summarizes this well by saying, "The covenant of grace was made with Christ as the second Adam, and in him with all the elect as his seed."[15]

The covenantal bond helps to explain why the unrighteousness of Adam and the righteousness of Christ are imputed or accounted to all who are in them. Adam was our representative in the covenant of works. Adam's disobedience not only introduced sin into the world (Rom. 5:12),

---

13. Matt. 26:28; Luke 1:68–72; Gal. 3:15–16; Heb. 8:6–13.

14. In Eph. 1:3, Paul wrote of "the God and Father of our Lord Jesus Christ," which is covenantal language similar to "the God of Abraham" or "the God of Israel." However, whereas the covenants with Abraham and Israel were instituted in human history, in v. 4 Paul indicated that we were chosen in Christ in eternity past. This implies an eternal covenant of grace instituted by God with Christ and the elect.

15. Quoted in *Westminster Confession of Faith* (Glasgow: Free Presbyterian Publications, 1994), 142.

but also brought judgment and condemnation upon all men (5:18). We all die because of Adam's sin. Paul proved this by pointing out in verse 14 that those who do not consciously transgress against a known commandment, as Adam did, still die. Otherwise, "sin is not imputed when there is no law" (Rom. 5:13). "Nevertheless death reigned from Adam to Moses" (5:14), and "the wages of sin is death" (Rom. 6:23). All mankind earned these horrible wages in Adam's transgression. Adam's sin counts against us because, as Thomas Boston says, there is "a moral bond between Adam and us: the bond of the covenant, which could be no other than the covenant of works."[16]

In the same way, Christ is our representative in the covenant of grace. Christ's obedience does not merely introduce holy living into the world, but brings "justification of life" as a "free gift" (5:18). This "gift of righteousness" (5:17) is not something we earn or work for, but is the righteous standing before God that Christ earned for us by his work. Thus Paul explains in Romans 3 and 4 that we are justified not by our works but by faith in Christ alone. Just as we die because of Adam's sin, so, when we are joined to Christ by true faith, we live because of Christ's obedience. Christ does not merely give us righteousness, but, as 1 Corinthians 1:30 tells us, Christ *is* our righteousness. And, as such, he is also our life (Col. 3:4).

The Second Adam's Resurrection unto Life

As the second Adam, Christ not only died for us but also rose again for us. Paul writes in 1 Corinthians 15:21–23,

---

16. *The Works of Thomas Boston*, 8:182, quoted in Philip Graham Ryken, *Thomas Boston as Preacher of the Fourfold State* (Carlisle, UK: Paternoster, 1999), 189.

For since by man came death, by man came also the resurrection of the dead. For as in Adam all die, even so in
Christ shall all be made alive. But every man in his own
order: Christ the firstfruits; afterward they that are Christ's
at his coming.

The "firstfruits" were the first crops to be harvested in any
given season, which God commanded Israel to offer to him
for his glory (Ex. 23:19; Lev. 23:10; Prov. 3:9). Christ was
offered to God for his glory, and he rose again as the "firstfruits" of the coming harvest, when all his people will rise to
meet him in the air (1 Thess. 4:13–18). Christ has inaugu-
rated a new day in the history of man, a day that began with
his own resurrection from the dead. As Herman Ridderbos
writes, "His resurrection represents the commencement of
the new world."[17]

In rising from the dead, Christ restored man to his God-
given position of honor and glory. God created men and women
to be kings and queens upon the earth. In Psalm 8, David
marvels that the God who created the sun and the stars pays
any attention to mortal man. In Psalm 8:5–6, he confesses
nonetheless,

Thou hast made him a little lower than the angels, and hast
crowned him with glory and honour.
Thou madest him to have dominion over the works of thy
hands; thou hast put all things under his feet.

17. "In the firstfruits the whole harvest becomes visible. So Christ is the Firstfruits of them that slept. In him the resurrection of the dead dawns, his resurrection
represents the commencement of the new world of God. . . . The expression 'the last
Adam' is again highly typical of the eschatological character of Paul's preaching:
Christ is thereby designated as the Inaugurator of the new humanity. . . . Christ
and Adam stand over against one another as the great representatives of the two
aeons, that of life and that of death" (Ridderbos, *Paul*, 56–57).

In Hebrews 2, Paul quotes this psalm and observes that at the present time we do not see all things put under the feet of mankind. The curse against Adam's sin continues to subject our world to futility and corruption (Rom. 8:20–21). "But," he says in Hebrews 2:9, "we see Jesus, who was made a little lower than the angels for the suffering of death, crowned with glory and honour." Now that Christ has risen from the dead and ascended into heaven to sit at God's right hand, far above all created principalities and powers, God is putting all things under his feet (Ps. 110:1; 1 Cor. 15:27; Eph. 1:20–22).

Christ rose higher than Adam ever stood. God raised him up and seated him at his right hand, and by our union with him, God has raised us up and seated us with him in heavenly places (Eph. 1:20; 2:6). Romans 5:17 says, "If by one man's offence death reigned by one; much more they which receive abundance of grace and of the gift of righteousness shall reign in life by one, Jesus Christ." As one commentator puts it, the slaves of death have become kings.[18] We must not miss the "much more" of Paul's argument (cf. 5:15). Christ has obtained for us a "superabundance of grace." The work of the second Adam abounds above and beyond the damage done by the sin of the first Adam. Not only did Christ open the door to paradise; it is now infinitely more glorious because of his enthronement in it (Pss. 2:6; 45:6). Christ not only returned to life but took hold of eternal, resurrection life (see more on that below).

The risen Christ is "the new man" (Eph. 2:15; 4:24). He rose from the dead as the prototype of the new humanity that God is raising up from the ruins of Adam's posterity. He is the pioneer or "captain" of our salvation (Heb. 2:10), who forges a

18. Leon Morris, *The Epistle to the Romans* (Grand Rapids: Eerdmans, 1988), 237.

way through death itself to enter into a new realm of life and draws us with him to follow where he leads.[19] This is why he rose on the first day of the week, which we celebrate as the Christian Sabbath or the Lord's Day. It was the first day of a new era for the human race. Christ is the firstborn of the new creation. His resurrection is the dawning of a new day for his people. In that new day, a believing sinner experiences a new life in Christ in every way. It is a new beginning with God, a new heart that provides new freedom in our Redeemer and Lord, so that we have new desires to do God's will and to be his willing servants.

What a hope we have! If the head is raised to glory, the members of the body will surely follow. We are the body of Christ. No wonder Paul reminds us, "Now is our salvation nearer than when we believed. The night is far spent, the day is at hand" (Rom. 13:11–12).

The Kingdom of the Second Adam

We have seen that God created Adam to reign as a king on the earth. God qualified Adam to reign by creating him in God's image. Genesis 1:26 says, "And God said, Let us make man in our image, after our likeness: and let them have dominion over the fish of the sea, and over the fowl of the air, and over the cattle, and over all the earth, and over every creeping thing that creepeth upon the earth." However, when Adam fell into sin, he became the slave of sin, and his reign gave way to the reign of Satan, sin, and death over the world. In Romans 5 and 6, Paul uses the word "reign," which is a kingdom word,[20] to describe

19. Peterson, *Salvation Accomplished by the Son*, 480, 497; Ridderbos, *Paul*, 56.
20. "Reign" (Greek, *basileuō*) is related to "kingdom" (*basileia*) and "king" (*basileus*).

how the bitter consequences of Adam's transgression reigned and ruled over mankind.[21]

In a similar but far more glorious way, the second Adam reigns over his kingdom in heaven and earth. The kingdom of the second Adam can be understood in terms of the recovery of the image of God, the reign of grace, the resurrection of the saints, and the reign of the saints over the new creation.

The Re-Creation of the Saints in God's Image

God reveals his eternal purpose for his people in Romans 8:29: "For whom he did foreknow, he also did predestinate to be conformed to the image of his Son, that he might be the firstborn among many brethren."[22] The incarnate Christ is the first member of a new family remade in his image. He is the Adam for a new human race renewed and reformed after the image of God.

Paul writes in Colossians 1:15 that Christ is "the image of the invisible God." On the one hand, Christ is the image of God because of his eternal nature as the Son of God, who is the brightness of God's glory and the express image of his person (Heb. 1:3; John 1:1, 14, 18). On the other hand, Christ is the image of God as the second Adam, that is, in his incarnation as a man and in his office as the Mediator.[23] The Devil attacked the image of God when he tempted Adam and his

21. Rom. 5:14, 17, 21; 6:12; see also Acts 26:18; Col. 1:13.
22. God's purpose is for *all* things, because he works all things for the good of those called according to his purpose (Rom. 8:28). He repeats the idea of "all things" in verses 32 and 37 and then offers an extensive list of good and bad experiences and powers in verses 38 and 39.
23. "Deeply embedded in such language [in Rom. 8:29] are the twin emphases, first, that the eternal Son of God perfectly bears the divine image and, second, that he did so in his own identity with us in our humanity. . . . This second matter—emphasis on Christ's humanity—is what is then picked up in our present passage with the phrase, 'the firstborn among many brothers and sisters'" (Gordon D. Fee, *Pauline Christology: An Exegetical-Theological Study* [Peabody, MA: Hendrickson,

wife. Christ, the righteous one, came to destroy the works of the Devil (1 John 3:7–8).

Christ is the human image of God sent to restore God's likeness in humanity. We have already seen how Christ exercised himself in obedience under extreme temptations. Although he never sinned under temptation, he nevertheless developed and strengthened his human righteousness, thus "learning obedience" through suffering (Heb. 4:15; 5:8). The same Holy Spirit who crafted and strengthened his humanity is now at work in us as the Spirit of Christ. John Calvin says that the Spirit of God is called "the Spirit of Christ" (Rom. 8:9), not only because the Spirit is linked to Christ in the Trinity, but also because he flows to us through Christ as the second Adam, so that Christ shares his life with us (1 Cor. 15:45).[24] Calvin writes that Christ is named "the Second Adam" because "he restores us to true and complete integrity [for] the end of regeneration is that Christ should reform us to God's image."[25]

All mankind possesses fragments of God's image, enough to make all human life sacred above the animals and worthy of honor and protection (Gen. 9:6; James 3:9–10; see also 1 Peter 2:17). However, these are but the ruins and remnants of the image that God created. Second Corinthians 4:4 says that the image of God in mankind is so broken and distorted by Satan that when we encounter God's true image in the gospel, we are utterly blind to God's glory shining in the person of his incarnate Son. We cannot see the glory of God in Christ

---

2007], 521). See also Peterson, *Salvation Accomplished by the Son*, 477, 489–90; Ridderbos, *Paul*, 69–78.

24. John Calvin, *Institutes of the Christian Religion*, ed. John T. McNeill, trans. Ford Lewis Battles (Philadelphia: Westminster Press, 1960), 3.1.2. For a summary of Calvin's view, see Robert A. Peterson Sr., *Calvin and the Atonement* (Ross-shire, UK: Christian Focus Publications, 1999), 61–68.

25. Calvin, *Institutes*, 1.15.4.

until, as 2 Corinthians 4:6 says, "God, who commanded the light to shine out of darkness, hath shined in our hearts, to give the light of the knowledge of the glory of God in the face of Jesus Christ." The first step in our becoming true image bearers of God is taken when the light of God's glory shines into our hearts. In an act of new creation accompanying the preaching of the gospel, the Holy Spirit opens our blind eyes and shows us the glory of Christ, the second Adam, and begins to transform us into the same glory (2 Cor. 3:17–18). Then, as converted people, our lifelong goal becomes to be transformed and remade in Christ's image. Calvin writes, "Just as our Lord Jesus is the second Adam, so he must be like a pattern to us, and we must be fashioned after him and his image, that we may be like him."[26]

In Christ, the ruins of God's image are rebuilt in three dimensions. We find one dimension in Colossians 3:10, "And have put on the new man, which is renewed in knowledge after the image of him that created him." We see two more in Ephesians 4:24, "And that ye put on the new man, which after God is created in righteousness and true holiness."[27] So when we are in Christ, the renewed image of God consists of renewal in knowledge, righteousness, and holiness. These three dimensions correspond to the threefold office of Christ as prophet, king, and priest.

- Christ came as our chief prophet and teacher, revealing the *knowledge* of God, and he trains us as prophets who know God and can make him known to others. We are

---

26. John Calvin, *Sermons on the Epistle to the Ephesians* (Edinburgh: Banner of Truth Trust, 1973), 434.

27. Literally, "righteousness and holiness of the truth," perhaps also indicating knowledge (truth).

his witnesses, his servants who declare that he alone is Lord. Let us speak up for the Lord, relying upon the Holy Spirit for boldness, wisdom, and love. Let us use our voices as family members, friends, church members, and citizens of our nation to advocate for God's name and God's law in our land.

- Christ came as our eternal King, who as "the Lord our *righteousness*" establishes righteousness and justice in the lives of his people.[28] By his grace, we too reign as righteous kings, the servants of the Lord empowered by the Spirit of the Lord to fight against sin and Satan and to do justice on the earth. Let us take up whatever authority God has given us as pastors, parents, and teachers, and as government officials, police officers, and owners or supervisors of businesses, to promote righteousness and exalt our nation, for sin is a shame to any people.

- Christ came as our only High Priest, opening the way of *holiness*, by which we draw near to God in worship, praise, and prayer.[29] Through his blood and mediation,

28. See Jer. 23:5–6. Of course, Paul can use the word "righteousness" (*dikaiosunē*) for the righteousness of Christ, imputed by faith (Rom. 3:21–22; Gal. 3:6). But here, as in Eph. 5:9, it refers to the life of justice infused by the Holy Spirit.

29. Here I am taking "holiness" to refer to covenantal piety toward God. The word "holiness" (Greek, *hosiotēs*) is not related to the New Testament term most often translated as "holy" (*hagios*). In the LXX, the first word or its cognate adjective (*hosios*) sometimes means "upright," as God is said to be "just and upright" (Hebrew, *yashar*, Deut. 32:4). If in Eph. 4:24 by "holiness" (*hosiotēs*) Paul means "moral uprightness," then its meaning largely overlaps with "righteousness." However, the term also refers to the "godly" one who calls upon the Lord and worships him according to his covenant (Hebrew, *hasid*, Pss. 4:3; 12:1; 30:4; 32:6; 50:5, and others). This is the far more common usage in the LXX (see *The New International Dictionary of New Testament Theology*, ed. Colin Brown [Grand Rapids: Zondervan, 1976], 2:237). If, therefore, Paul has in view covenantal piety, then it has a distinctly godward focus and "righteousness" may refer to justice in one's dealings with men.

we too serve God as priests by our prayers, by offering ourselves to him as living sacrifices, and by offering the sacrifice of praise, "the fruit of our lips giving thanks to his name" (Heb. 4:16; Rom. 12:1; Heb. 13:15). Our whole life becomes an act of worship, and in public worship with the church we have a foretaste of heaven (Heb. 12:22–24). Let us therefore ground our public lives in private devotion, seeking the Lord in his Word, by fervent prayer and by patiently suffering under God's providence so that his kingdom may come and his will may be done.

We may not push ahead with selfish ambition and triumphal arrogance. I am not talking about legalism and hypocrisy. The way to follow our second Adam is to deny ourselves, take up our cross, and serve one another in love, suffering the cost while persevering in hope. But the victory of the second Adam reminds us that we live under the reign of grace, not the tyranny of sin. Paul closes his treatment of the two Adams in Romans 5 with these glowing words: "But where sin abounded, grace did much more abound: that as sin hath reigned unto death, even so might grace reign through righteousness unto eternal life by Jesus Christ our Lord" (Rom. 5:20–21).

Our great confidence as we seek to serve God is that, in Christ, our God has re-created us in the image of God so that we can do good works that are pleasing to him. Ephesians 2:10 says, "For we are his workmanship, created in Christ Jesus unto good works, which God hath before

---

The godward focus fits well with its use with respect to godly prayer (1 Tim. 2:8) and Christ as priest (Heb. 7:26), and as a man who rejoiced confidently in the Lord (Acts 2:27 and 13:34–35, both quoting Ps. 16:10).

ordained that we should walk in them." Let us therefore press on to serve the Lord, trusting that our second Adam blazed the trail ahead of us, and that by grace we follow in his footsteps. Yes, and we will follow him all the way to his kingdom of glory.

The Resurrection of the Saints in Glory

Christ is the firstborn from the dead (Col. 1:18). His resurrection life is the life of his people (Col. 3:1–4). He is renewing us now in the inner man, and he will transform our vile bodies to be like his glorious body (Phil. 3:21). We cannot fully know or understand what we will be as spirits made perfect, dwelling in bodies clad with immortality and incorruption, but we know that we will be like him because we will see him as he is (1 John 3:2). Eternal life is not just our present condition extended forever; eternal life is a different mode of life than we have ever known. Our present bodies are just the seed of our future life (1 Cor. 15:37). The resurrection will bring to our bodies a heavenly glory that transcends our present experience as much as the angels in heaven presently transcend men on earth (Luke 20:34–36; 1 Cor. 15:47–48).

Paul explained this in a series of contrasts in 1 Corinthians 15:42–43,

> So also is the resurrection of the dead. It is sown in corruption; it is raised in incorruption: it is sown in dishonour; it is raised in glory: it is sown in weakness; it is raised in power: it is sown a natural body; it is raised a spiritual body. There is a natural body, and there is a spiritual body.

Consider these contrasts one by one:

- Fallen men and women suffer "corruption" in the form of pain, disease, handicaps, old age, and ultimately death and decay. This is our legacy from the first Adam: "Dust thou art, and unto dust shalt thou return" (Gen. 3:19). But the second Adam will free us from all this misery: "There shall be no more death, neither sorrow, nor crying, neither shall there be any more pain" (Rev. 21:4). There will be no more arthritis, no more broken bones, no more gunshot wounds or improvised explosive devices, no more knee replacements, no more cancer—only life to the fullest measure. We will truly be immortal, as men have dreamed for ages.

- Fallen people experience "dishonour"—embarrassment and shame because of our sins, guilt, foolishness, and stupidity and the ugliness and deformity of our bodies. But the second Adam will raise us in glory, in radiant beauty in God's kingdom: "Then shall the righteous shine forth as the sun" (Matt. 13:43). Christ will crown us with glory, publicly commend us for our service, and reward every cup of cold water that we have given in service to him.

- Fallen people are frustrated by "weakness"—the severe limitations that our brains and bodies place upon us, so that we grow weary, make mistakes, and lack the strength and endurance to do what we desire. Christ will give us power to be youthful, dynamic, quick, and energetic. We will never have to drag ourselves out of bed or have someone push us around in a wheelchair. We will spread our wings and soar as eagles in all that we do (Ps. 103:5; Isa. 40:31).

- As fallen beings, our bodies possess only a "natural" life like the animals.[30] In verse 50, Paul says that, as

30. The word "natural" (*psychikos*) is derived from "soul" or "life" (*psychē*). The latter may refer to the human soul, but it may also be used of the life animating

such, our "flesh and blood cannot inherit the kingdom of God." But Christ will raise us from the dead
with "spiritual" bodies—that is, bodies transformed
and enlivened by the Holy Spirit. We will experience
a new order of life, kingdom life, "living from divine
power."[31] We will no longer have "natural" bodies,
but "supernatural" bodies—that is, bodies quickened
with the supernatural life of the Holy Spirit."[32] This
seems to be what Paul means in verse 45, "The last
Adam was made a quickening spirit."[33] Christ "hath
abolished death, and hath brought life and immortality to light through the gospel" (2 Tim. 1:10). Christ
rose bodily from the dead, but he rose in the power
of the Holy Spirit to give life to our mortal bodies
by that same Spirit (Rom. 1:4; 8:11). Who can say
what pleasure and power we will experience when the
Holy Spirit becomes our source of life (Ps. 16:11)?
God himself will be our food, our drink, our breath,
and our very life, and we will enjoy him forever and
ever (Ps. 73:26).

---

the bodies of animals (Gen. 1:20, 21, 24, 30; 2:19 LXX). The same expression used
of such a "living creature" (*psychē zōsa*) is quoted from Gen. 2:7 (LXX) by Paul
in 1 Cor. 15:45 about Adam in contrast to Christ. So it seems that the contrast is
between animal life and the indwelling Holy Spirit.

31. Ridderbos, *Paul*, 544.

32. Fee, *Pauline Christology*, 516–17.

33. "Quickening" (participle of *zōopoieō*) means "life-giving." Adam was
created as a "living creature," but Christ rose as the "life-giving Spirit," implying
that the resurrection life consists of an indwelling principle of life from the Spirit
within the body of resurrected man, just as he presently supplies an indwelling principle of life in the soul of the regenerate man. The contrast between
"natural" and "spiritual" also appears in 1 Cor. 2:12–3:3, where it is a contrast
between those who are not experiencing the influence of the Holy Spirit and
those illuminated and renewed by him. See Peterson, *Salvation Accomplished
by the Son*, 482–83.

The Reign of the Saints with Christ

God created Adam to reign in a covenant relationship with him. I noted earlier how Genesis 1:26 links the image of God in Adam to Adam's kingdom or exercise of dominion over all the creatures of the sea, sky, and earth. Genesis 5:1–3 also reveals that God's image meant that Adam was created to be God's son. That passage says that just as God created Adam in his likeness, so, in turn, Adam begat a son in his likeness. God made Adam to rule over the world as the son of God (Luke 3:38), knowing his Creator not just as the divine Creator but also as his covenant Lord and Father.

We catch glimpses of the intimate, childlike friendship that Adam enjoys with God in Genesis 2, as God brings the animals to Adam to be named and then forms the woman and brings her to Adam as his companion. Genesis 2 closes with the divine Father, his human son Adam, and his human daughter, Adam's bride, in Paradise. This is a picture of Christ's kingdom, in which the members of the church of God enjoy fellowship with their heavenly Father in and through the person and work of his incarnate Son (1 John 1:3).

The apostle Paul quotes Genesis 2:24 at the end of Ephesians 5. The Genesis 2 text is about the marriage or "joining" of the man and the woman. Surprisingly, however, in Ephesians 5:32 Paul applies this text to Christ and the church: "This is a great mystery: but I speak concerning Christ and the church." If Christ is the second Adam, then the church is Christ's bride, created by God to reign with his Son in the new paradise. The ultimate goal of our redemption by Christ is to live with him in the spiritual bond of holy matrimony. Ephesians 5:27 says that Christ died for the church, "that he might present it to himself a glorious church, not having spot, or wrinkle, or any such thing; but that it should be holy and without blemish." As the members of that church, we will be perfectly pleasing and delightful to the Lord in every way.

This matrimonial vision is the grand theme of the last chapters of the book of Revelation: the solemnization of the long-anticipated marriage of Christ to his bride, and their life together under the Father's blessing in paradise. But instead of Adam, there is "the Lamb," our Lord Jesus, who laid down his life to buy us with his blood. We will return to paradise to drink from "a pure river of water of life, clear as crystal, proceeding out of the throne of God and of the Lamb," and to eat of "the tree of life, which bare twelve manner of fruits, and yielded her fruit every month: and the leaves of the tree were for the healing of the nations" (Rev. 22:1–4).

We will enjoy the Father's presence and blessing when God at last dwells with men and when we inherit the promise that "he that overcometh shall inherit all things; and I will be his God, and he shall be my son" (Rev. 21:3, 6–7). We will live in paradise, married to our second Adam—not naked, but clothed in his righteousness, "for the marriage of the Lamb is come, and his wife hath made herself ready. And to her was granted that she should be arrayed in fine linen, clean and white: for the fine linen is the righteousness of saints"—"Blessed are they which are called unto the marriage supper of the Lamb" (Rev. 19:6–9)! We will be enthroned with Christ in the new heaven and the new earth, where the Lord God will be our light, and we "shall reign for ever and ever" (Rev. 22:5), eternally beholding his face—no longer through "a glass, darkly; but then face to face" (1 Cor. 13:12). In some ways, the last chapter of the Bible contains the most stunning verse in all of Scripture: "And they shall see his face" (Rev. 22:4)! Have you ever considered the amazing wonder of this? The Scriptures teach repeatedly that no man shall see God's face and live; the righteous angels cover their faces with their wings as they gaze upon the Deity in celestial bliss. But one day in glory, all of us believers—sinners worthy of hell in ourselves—will be perfect brides and be able to behold our Bridegroom face to face. He will exult that he sees no sin in us—no sin in his Jacob and no transgression in his Israel. Oh, eternal wonder—to be sin-free in Immanuel's land!

Thus the Bible ends where it began, but the music is transposed to a much higher key. We will return to paradise, but we will find one there who was not seen in the earthly Eden: the incarnate, crucified, risen, and glorified Christ. And we will be with him—yes, married to him and gazing upon him—forever in the heavenly paradise! That is real, eternal utopia!

Conclusion

As we have considered Christ, the second Adam, we have seen the King in his beauty. How beautiful is Christ! Behold, he is lovely—our beloved—yes, delightful. He has brought us to the banqueting house, and his banner over us is love (Song 2:4). Love brought him down from heaven to embrace our weak human nature. Love led him into the wilderness to fast for forty days and to suffer fierce temptation. Love drew him to the cross, where his obedience would cover our shame and clothe our nakedness. Love broke the chains of death and brought him out of the grave to bless us. Love showers down on us from his heavenly throne in all the graces of the Spirit. Love will bring him back again to take us to be with him in paradise. The doctrine of Christ, the second Adam, is a love story that stretches from the first creation to the new creation. It is the truest happily-ever-after story ever written, for it was written by God himself.

If you were to boil down all that we have seen from Scripture and condense it into one statement, it would be this: *Christ is the second Adam upon whom all our hope depends.* In Christ we have a hope of glory that surpasses anything that money can buy or science can discover for us in this world. Christ is the treasure hidden in the field, so valuable that those who discover it are glad to part with everything they have if that is what it takes to gain him. The work of the second Adam is a sparkling diamond worth more than all the riches of this world. Indeed, it is the diamond in the wedding ring that is the sign of our marriage to God himself in a relationship of eternal love.

This doctrine opens up a crucial question, however. Do you belong to Christ? Have you escaped the deadly legacy of the first Adam, in whom all die? Do you belong to Christ as the second Adam, in whom all shall be made alive?

We put on Christ and his perfect righteousness, the wedding ring and the wedding garment, by a Spirit-worked faith in Christ. There is no other way. Faith is the receiving of Christ with all his benefits. Romans 5:17 says, "For if by one man's offence death reigned by one; much more they which receive abundance of grace and of the gift of righteousness shall reign in life by one, Jesus Christ." Mark those words: *they which receive.* Have you received this second Adam? He is wooing you even now through the preaching of his Word. The Spirit and the bride say, "Come." Let the one who hears say, "Come." And let the one who thirsts for the life that only the second Adam can give take the water of life freely.

The Contrast between the First and Second Adams

The Work of the First Adam	The Work of the Second Adam
Law and temptation	Law and temptation
Disobedience while living in Paradise	Obedience unto death upon the cross
Condemnation and death	Justification and resurrection life

The People of the First Adam	The People of the Second Adam
One man acting for all who are in him	One man acting for all who are in him
Our representative in the covenant of works	Our surety in the covenant of grace
Union with him by ordinary generation	Union with him by the Spirit's regeneration

The Kingdom of the First Adam	The Kingdom of the Second Adam
Original creation in God's image	New creation in God's image
Kingdom of sin and misery	Kingdom of grace and life
Reign over all things on earth	Reign over all things in heaven and on earth

9

From God's Garden to God's City

RICHARD D. PHILLIPS

*And I heard a loud voice from the throne saying,
"Behold, the dwelling place of God is with man. He
will dwell with them, and they will be his people,
and God himself will be with them as their God."*
(Revelation 21:3)

ONE OF THE TOP movies in 2012 was the film adaptation of J. R. R. Tolkien's *The Hobbit*. The enduring popularity of Tolkien's fantasy tales bears testimony to the way he connects with the true story of our world. *The Hobbit* tells of a group of warrior dwarfs whose home was lost to the assault of a terrible dragon. Once, their mountain kingdom had been the wonder of the world, and their wealth had seemed unending. They dwelt in the splendor of gold and jewels. But now their paradise has been lost, and they are forced to wander the world in poverty and weakness. This presents an analogy to the state of the entire human race since the fall of Adam and our expulsion from the garden of Eden.

Early in the movie there is a conversation between the dwarf leader, Thorin Oakenshield, and one of his older relatives, Balin. The older dwarf argues the futility of Thorin's plan to return to the mountain kingdom and regain his throne. Balin says, "What are we? Merchants, miners, tinkers, toy makers. Hardly the stuff of legend."[1] So it is for mankind after the fall. We look back in Genesis to the glory of our creation in the image of God. Once we dwelt in the garden paradise. We walked with the Lord God "in the cool of the day" (Gen. 3:8). Mankind exercised glorious dominion over the earth in the splendor of original righteousness. But sin came, like the dragon that swept down upon the mountain of dwarfs. Transgression made a ruin of our once-glorious condition, leaving us cast out to drift in the dust of the world. "What are we?" we now ask. Businessmen, teachers, plumbers, and bakers. Hardly the stuff of glory.

The value of our study of the biblical doctrine of creation is that it tells us what we were created to be, reminding us of our original dignity, righteousness, and fellowship with God. But, as Balin told the dwarf prince Thorin, the reality is that we can never go back. Christians look back on creation as a paradise lost, to which we will never return.

The question, then, is whether Adam's fall leaves us cut off from our original destiny. Is getting by in this life the best we can do? Is there a hope of glory for us? The book of Revelation answers by directing our gaze forward. We will

---

1. "Difficult Decision," *The Hobbit: An Unexpected Journey*, directed by Peter Jackson (2012; Burbank, CA: Warner Home Video, 2013), DVD.

never again see the original creation. But as we have union with Christ, the Redeemer, in faith, there is a new creation, a renewed heaven and earth at which we are destined to arrive. The last book of the Bible thus answers the plight of the Bible's first book. The garden that was lost in the beginning is replaced by the glorious city of God at the end of this age. Revelation 21:1 lifts up our eyes to see a vision designed to lift us out of our mundane worldliness: "Then I saw a new heaven and a new earth, for the first heaven and the first earth had passed away."

The glory of the Bible's completed story is that in the glorious city of the renewed world at the end, all that was lost in the garden's fall is regained, redeemed, and restored to the splendor originally designed for it to become. God told Adam and Eve in the garden to "be fruitful and multiply and fill the earth and subdue it" (Gen. 1:28). Where Adam failed, the second Adam, Jesus Christ, fulfilled this mandate for history. The final chapters of the Bible present his eternal achievement. Revelation 21:1 says that in the new heaven and the new earth "the sea was no more," referring to the defeat of God's enemies, together with all evil, darkness, and fear. Revelation 21:2 describes "the holy city, new Jerusalem, coming down out of heaven from God, prepared as a bride adorned for her husband." This foretells the blessing of Christ's glorified people in the perfection of holiness and righteousness that will be theirs in the end. Verse 4 tells of the eradication of the cursed effects of sin and the fall. All the sorrow that resulted from sin will have no place in the city to come: "He will wipe away every tear from their eyes, and death shall be no more, neither shall there be mourning nor crying nor pain anymore, for the former things have passed away." This addresses the three chief features of man's fallen condition: our evil spiritual enemy, our condemnation for the guilt and corruption of sin, and the misery of life in a world stalked by death and futility. With these three gone, God's original covenant aim for creation is achieved: "Behold, the dwelling place of God is with man. He will dwell with them, and they will be his people, and God himself will be with them as their God" (Rev. 21:3).

No More Sea

The opening statement of verse 1 provides some of the greatest encouragement that Christians could ever receive: "Then I saw a new heaven and a new earth, for the first heaven and the first earth had passed away." The Bible states that when Christ returns, "the heavens and the earth," which is a way of referring to the entire universe, will be cleansed and renewed in glory. Paul says, "The creation itself will be set free from its bondage to corruption and obtain the freedom of the glory of the children of God" (Rom. 8:21).

Some Christians teach a doctrine in which the present universe is consumed and replaced by a new one, largely on the basis of Peter's second epistle. Peter says that just as the world of Noah was destroyed by the flood, when Jesus returns "the heavens will pass away with a roar, and the heavenly bodies will be burned up and dissolved, and the earth and the works that are done on it will be exposed" (2 Peter 3:10). This passage is understood to teach the eradication of this present world and its replacement by a new one.

A better understanding is that after Christ returns, the cosmos will be cleansed and renewed. Instead of making "all new things," Christ makes "all things new." In Matthew 19:28, Jesus speaks of "the new world" after he returns. In Greek, the word is the *palingenesia*, that is, the "regeneration," suggesting an analogy between the spiritual rebirth of believers in coming to Jesus and the transformation of heaven and earth after Jesus returns. The contrary idea, that Christ eliminates the original creation because of sin, has alarming implications. In this view, Satan will succeed in overthrowing the glorious work of God recorded in Genesis 1. Moreover, if God eradicates the present heavens and earth, then, as Cornelis P. Venema writes, "we would have to conclude that the Triune God's redemptive work discards rather than renews all things."[2]

If Christ's return renews rather than replaces the universe, how do we understand Peter's statement that "the heavens will pass away" and "the heavenly bodies will be burned up and dissolved" (2 Peter 3:10)? The answer is seen in Peter's analogy to the destruction of the flood in Noah's time. The great flood did not destroy the world itself but rather removed sinners in judgment and cleansed the world of corruption. Just as Noah stepped out of the ark into a renewed version of the old world, with sin swept away, so Christ will usher his church into a creation that has been cleansed and made glorious. As Venema writes, "Once more, but now in a surpassing way, the creation will be a temple fit for the dwelling of God with his people."[3]

Revelation 21:1 makes a provocative statement that provides our first point of emphasis: "And the sea was no more." In this book, we have been arguing for the literal, historical reading of Genesis 1. But Revelation is a book of symbolic presentations of history. The point of the sea is not the

2. Cornelis P. Venema, *The Promise of the Future* (Edinburgh: Banner of Truth, 2000), 461.
3. Ibid., 460.

topography of the new creation; rather, the sea represents the realm of evil and rebellion against God. Psalm 74 describes salvation as God breaking the head of "the sea monsters" and crushing "Leviathan," the great mythical sea monster that represents idolatrous opposition to God (vv. 12–14). James Hamilton writes that for the Israelites the sea was "the great dark unknown from which evil comes."[4] This provides the answer to the question, "What is the shortest book in all history?" The answer is, "Naval heroes of ancient Israel." There are no naval heroes in Israel, because God's covenant people avoided the sea as a symbol of chaos and a source of destruction. Isaiah 27:1 says that God "will slay the dragon that is in the sea." In Revelation 13:1, Satan, the dragon, raises up his beast "out of the sea." When Christ returns to judge in Revelation 20:10, Satan and his beast are cast into a lake that is consumed with eternal fire and sulfur.

How we rejoice that Christ has triumphed, so that in the new creation "the sea was no more" (Rev. 21:1)! The New Testament tells of Christ systematically crushing each of his enemies. Jesus conquered sin by his righteous life, atoning death on the cross, and glorious resurrection from the grave. Christ has destroyed the reign of Satan by his conquest of sin! Paul writes that "God has put all things in subjection under his feet" (1 Cor. 15:27), so Christians even now look to Jesus and see the certainty of his complete victory. In terms of the images of Revelation, the new world will be completely free from the dragon, his beasts, the false prophet, and the harlot, together with their wicked program. Even the sea, the realm of chaos from which they came, will be no more.

4. James M. Hamilton Jr., *Revelation: The Spirit Speaks to the Churches* (Wheaton, IL: Crossway, 2012), 383.

Although we still struggle with sin and evil, the day is coming soon in the renewed world when they will be removed. The prophets anticipated that day with joyful wonder. Isaiah wrote,

> The wolf shall dwell with the lamb,
>   and the leopard shall lie down with the young goat,
> and the calf and the lion and the fattened calf together;
>   and a little child shall lead them. (Isa. 11:6)

> They shall not hurt or destroy
>   in all my holy mountain;
> for the earth shall be full of the knowledge of the LORD
>   as the waters cover the sea. (Isa. 11:9)

The Bible shows this vision to us now to make a point. It is wrong for a Christian to say, "We are just sinners like everyone else. We are hardly the stuff of legends." In fact, that is precisely what we are. We are the future heirs of glory—still living east of Eden, to be sure, but destined for a new world in which the sea is no more. For this reason, Paul urges the Ephesians never to become partners with the agents of evil. He explains, "For at one time you were darkness, but now you are light in the Lord." We are the stuff of biblical legend! Therefore, "walk as children of light (for the fruit of light is found in all that is good and right and true), and try to discern what is pleasing to the Lord" (Eph. 5:7–10).

Do you feel overcome by sin, either your own sins or the sins of the world pressing around you? Do you feel like you are about to go under, to drown in the sea of commonplace iniquity? Look ahead to the new world that is ahead of you if you simply walk in discipleship with Christ. You are light in the Lord, a child of light! The sea will be no more. So do not give in to temptation; do not compromise with the evils of spiritual

175

darkness. Take no part in them, and rejoice in awaiting the new creation, where there will be no transgression, no evil rebellion, and no temptation to sin.

The Glorified, Righteous Bride

We see the second feature of our fallen world, our condemnation for sin, removed from the church in the new creation ushered in at Christ's return: "And I saw the holy city, new Jerusalem, coming down out of heaven from God, prepared as a bride adorned for her husband" (Rev. 21:2). We are reminded here that the Bible does not depict the end of history with Christians "going to heaven," but with the church dwelling in the eternal holy city, new Jerusalem, coming down out of heaven into the renewed cosmos. And the church will be clean and beautiful— "prepared as a bride adorned for her husband."

The old world in which we now live, the world of the paradise lost, is stalked by the evil dragon with his beasts, false prophets, and harlot seducers (see Rev. 12–17). We have fallen prey to their wiles, becoming corrupted by shameful sins and being condemned for the guilt of our sin in God's sight. In this, too, Christ has the victory in purchasing and cleansing a bride for himself, the church, consisting of all who believe on him. By offering an atoning sacrifice in his blood, Jesus has cleansed us from all sin, gaining our eternal forgiveness before God, which we receive through faith alone. We have, Paul says, "redemption through his blood, the forgiveness of our trespasses, according to the riches of his grace" (Eph. 1:7).

A great picture of the cleansing of sinners to be the people of God is found in Zechariah 3. The prophet saw "Joshua the high priest standing before the angel of the LORD, and Satan standing at his right hand to accuse him" (Zech. 3:1). The high priest represented all of Israel, which had returned to Jerusalem from its exile in Babylon, where Israel had been punished for its sin. Now that faithful believers had returned to the Lord, Satan accused them by pointing out the failed spiritual legacy Joshua represented. But the Lord answered him: "The LORD said to Satan, 'The LORD rebuke you, O Satan!'" (v. 2). Zechariah adds, "Now Joshua was standing before the angel, clothed with filthy garments" (v. 3). How could the Lord rebuke the accusing Satan if Joshua was in fact dressed in the filthiness of his sins? The answer is given in the next verse: the angel, representing Christ, says, "Remove the filthy garments from him." To Joshua he says, "Behold, I have taken your iniquity away from you, and I will clothe you with pure vestments" (v. 4). So it is for the church as "a bride adorned for her husband" (Rev. 21:2). Christ took away her filthy garments and put them on himself when he suffered God's wrath on the cross. He then placed his own righteousness on her, as a glorious wedding dress in which to enter eternity with him. Therefore, Isaiah 62:5 says to Christians, "As the bridegroom rejoices over the bride, so shall your God rejoice over you."

Is it true, then, that Christians are just like others, not the stuff of legend? We are the bride of God the Son, having been cleansed by his blood on the cross and justified to dwell in his love forever.

What do brides do as they await their wedding? They beautify themselves. So we now are to seek the beauty of holiness. Christ himself is laboring in us to this end:

> that he might sanctify her, having cleansed her by the washing of water with the word, so that he might present the church to himself in splendor, without spot or wrinkle or any such thing, that she might be holy and without blemish. (Eph. 5:26–27)

This is our destiny, and now we prepare for it and grow in sanctification so as to present ourselves to the embrace of our Savior Lord.

An End to Sorrow and Death

When we think of the ravages of this present evil age, we think of our spiritual enemies and our own corruption and guilt in sin. Christ is the victor over both of these, and the new age awaiting us will be free from it all. But Revelation 21:4 points out a third consequence of our fall: our life under the curse and misery of sorrow and death. "He will wipe away every tear from their eyes, and death shall be no more, neither shall there be mourning nor crying nor pain anymore, for the former things have passed away."

I am getting to be old enough that death is more and more a part of my life. Both of my parents have died, and I miss them greatly. People I know who are dying are getting closer to my age all the time, and I am increasingly faced with the near prospect of the end of my own life. The wear and tear of fallen life brings tears to the eyes. I have gone through deep periods of mourning. Moreover, life seems to be slipping by more quickly. Not long ago I was driving to a meeting in Philadelphia, and on the way I drove up the street where my wife and I bought our first house when our children were little. There was the park with the big green turtle they played on. There was the driveway where they rode tricycles. It brought tears to my eyes, because those days are gone. I realize more than ever that the sweet things of today will soon slip away. This is true for the whole of our experience. Time and death stalk all who live in this present world. But the age to come will know no death nor sorrow nor tears nor pain anymore.

One of my favorite funeral texts is Psalm 116. Its most famous verse says, "Precious in the sight of the LORD is the death of his saints" (v. 15). But my favorite is verse 9: "I will walk before the LORD in the land of the living." It is the life after this world that is the land of the living. We inhabit the land of the dying. But when Christ returns, those who are joined to him through faith will all have eternal life. It is in that new world that the grief we bear in this world will finally be put away, and our tears will be wiped by God from our cheeks.

In John Bunyan's *Pilgrim's Progress*, early in his pilgrimage Christian is taken to the house Beautiful. From there he can look far ahead and see Immanuel's Land, where the blessings he seeks can be found. In Revelation 21:4, God's hand reaches to us now to wipe away our tears and let us know that the time will come when Christ has returned and grief will be no more. Encouraged by his grace, we face the sorrows of this life with courage, undeterred in our pilgrimage toward the promised land of glory ahead.

Dwelling Forever with God

There is so much for us to look forward to in the new creation that will arrive with Jesus Christ. The vision of Revelation 21 is intended to strengthen our legs and renew our gospel journey. We look back to creation to remember who we are and what our destiny is. Yet we can never return to the garden where Adam walked with God in the cool of the day. But we can turn our face toward the future, awaiting "our blessed hope, the appearing of the glory of our great God and Savior Jesus Christ" (Titus 2:13).

So far, the picture of the new creation in Revelation 21:1–4 has been primarily negative. There will be no sea, no guilt for sin or stain of iniquity, and no weeping or sorrow. Yet at the heart of this passage is the great positive blessing awaiting Christ's people there: "And I heard a loud voice from the throne saying, 'Behold, the dwelling place of God is with man. He will dwell with them, and they will be his people, and God himself will be with them as their God'" (v. 3). William Hendriksen describes this as "the climax of that entire process whereby God comes to His people. So close is this eternal communion between God and His elect that He, as it were, dwells with them in one tent—His tent, the glory of His attributes."[5]

The voice speaking from God's throne literally says, "The tabernacle of God is with men, and he will tabernacle with them." This fulfills the promise given in Ezekiel 37:26–27, which looks ahead to the time when God's Spirit would come through the new and everlasting covenant in Christ: "I . . . will set my sanctuary in their midst forevermore. My dwelling place shall be with them, and I will be their God, and they shall be my people." Simon Kistemaker calls this promise "a golden thread woven into the fabric of Scripture from beginning to end."[6] God promised to Abraham that he would establish "an everlasting covenant, to be God to you and to your offspring after you" (Gen. 17:7). This was God's purpose in the founding of Israel: "I will take you to be my people, and I will be your God" (Ex. 6:7). When God commanded Moses to construct the tabernacle in the desert, he said, "I will make my dwelling among you. . . . And I will walk among you and will be your God, and you shall be my people" (Lev. 26:11–12). Jesus fulfilled this promise in part by

5. William Hendriksen, *More Than Conquerors: An Interpretation of the Book of Revelation* (Grand Rapids: Baker, 1967), 199.
6. Simon J. Kistemaker, *Revelation* (Grand Rapids: Baker, 2001), 557.

his incarnation: "And the Word became flesh and dwelt among us, and we have seen his glory" (John 1:14).

Christians enjoy greater privileges than God's people knew in the Old Testament. Then only Moses and the high priests could enter God's tabernacle and see his glory, whereas now God's glory tabernacles in the heart of every believer through the Holy Spirit (2 Cor. 3:18). Our privileges will be greater in eternity than Adam and Eve knew in the garden before the fall. In the age to come, the longing of every spirit to know God and see his face will be perfectly fulfilled. The communion that God has eternally purposed to enjoy with his people will be achieved.

Here is the final realization of the Aaronic blessing:

> The Lord bless you and keep you;
> the Lord make his face to shine upon you and be gracious
> to you;
> the Lord lift up his countenance upon you and give you
> peace. (Num. 6:24–26)

Venema writes that when Christ's redeeming work is fully completed, the life to come "will consist in finding joy in God, living before his face. . . . Believers will stand unbowed before God, confident again in his presence that they are acceptable to him. The smile of God's countenance will shine upon the glorified members of Christ throughout all eternity."[7]

The Stuff of Legend

Are you still so sure that you are not the stuff of legend? Are you just a merchant, miner, tinker, or toy maker, as Balin says

7. Venema, *The Promise of the Future*, 482–83.

to Prince Thorin in *The Hobbit*? The Bible says you are children of light, children of God, heirs of eternal glory.

We have been studying creation and its glory in the studies of this book, finding the dignity of our race in Adam along with our tragedy in his fall. We cannot go back to the garden. But we can go forward to the Holy City. In fact, she is presently among us in the communion of the Christian church. Are you committed to her? Are you serving the gospel cause within her? Are you beautifying the church—that is, yourself and fellow believers—through ministry of the Word, prayer, and sacraments to present yourselves holy to Christ? That gives meaning to every life.

The story that creation begins with Adam and Eve in the glory of the paradise that they lost is concluded in the redemption glory of Revelation 21 and 22. There we see a holy city, a beautiful bride, a tearless everlasting life, and a loving divine Savior who awaits the consummation of our love. Who will be there? All who confess their sins, trust in the blood of Christ, and believe in the gospel of his salvation.

In his first epistle, the apostle John gives a fitting conclusion, putting our calling in perhaps its most eloquent and moving form: looking back on creation lost, looking forward to the new creation to come, and looking to Christ in faith for a present salvation.

> See what kind of love the Father has given to us, that we should be called children of God; and so we are. The reason why the world does not know us is that it did not know him. Beloved, we are God's children now, and what we will be has not yet appeared; but we know that when he appears we will be like him, because we shall see him as he is. And everyone who thus hopes in him purifies himself as he is pure. (1 John 3:1–3)

10

Original Sin and Modern Theology

CARL R. TRUEMAN

TO WRITE A CHAPTER on original sin in modern theology is no easy task. The problem is essentially one of selection: modern theology is such a diverse phenomenon that it is impossible to do justice to the range of opinions on this, or indeed any other doctrinal locus, in any kind of comprehensive way even in survey form. Indeed, modern theology, having lost its unifying foundation in a divinely inspired Bible, has become in the past fifty years little more than a function of wider identity politics. Theologians rarely produce dogmatic theology in terms of its classical structure: now we have feminist theology, queer theology, black theology, and so on. Each of these streams may well have interesting things to say, but their very existence points to the problem of how to address any single topic or how to select "representative" theologians. That which is representative to one might be a pitiful aberration to another.

Thus, in this chapter I make no claims to provide a comprehensive account of original sin in modern theology. Instead, I have chosen to survey six mainline (i.e., not conservative evangelical) theologians who have been influential on various strands of modern thought. I also consider these examples to reflect the broad contours and emphases of approaches to original sin in a theological world that has by and large decided that Adam and Eve never existed and that the fall was not an event in history that moved the created realm from a position of integrity to that of being under the curse of God. These selected theologians allow us to see what is at stake theologically in the current debates over human origins and creation.[1]

The three figures who occupy most space in the subsequent pages are Friedrich Schleiermacher, Walter Rauschenbusch, and Karl Barth. The choice of Schleiermacher really needs no justification: he is the father of modern liberalism and the classic representative of attempts to rebuild Christianity in light of the Enlightenment, and specifically Kantian, critique. Rauschenbusch may be a more surprising choice, but his theology of the social gospel surely represents the most significant application of a basically Schleiermacherian approach to original sin in the English-speaking world, and with his emphasis on the social nature of such sin, he stands in positive connection to much of subsequent liberal theology. Karl Barth, like Schleiermacher, is an obvious choice, representing the most significant dogmatic

1. I have also chosen only Protestant theologians. Roman Catholics have continued to address the issues of sin and original sin, but I am working on the assumption that this volume is aimed primarily at a Protestant evangelical readership and thus have focused my attention on those thinkers who are most likely to be of significance to those in that tradition. Further, I have not addressed any liberation, black, feminist, or queer theologians. This is not because such have not made significant contributions to the theological field, but because they all by and large stand on the same side of the theological divide relative to the orthodox tradition on Adam and sin as those represented here.

voice of the twentieth century and the most significant critical respondent to Schleiermacher who yet accepted fundamental elements of the Enlightenment critique of his great foe.

The choice of Rudolf Bultmann, Reinhold Niebuhr, and Wolfhart Pannenberg is perhaps more personal. As noted above, the last century has produced an ever more variegated crop of theologians and theologies. Yet these three men certainly represent key figures: Bultmann was to biblical scholarship what Barth was to dogmatics; Niebuhr represents a heady mix of social gospel and pessimism, which separated him from both the kind of theology espoused by Rauschenbusch and that of Barth; and Pannenberg is perhaps the latest, and maybe the last, attempt to articulate a full system of theology in the classic liberal tradition.

Friedrich Schleiermacher (1768–1834)

As with so much modern theology, the basic terms of debate were set by the great German theologian Friedrich Schleiermacher in the nineteenth century. In the wake of the Enlightenment and works such as Pierre Bayle's encyclopedia, the doctrine of original sin had become both distasteful and a matter of ridicule and consequently dropped from theological discourse.[2] Schleiermacher, however, attempted a major reconstruction of Christian doctrine that took seriously the great themes of Christian dogmatics while yet subjecting them to searching criticism and significant revision. One might summarize his

2. Of course, opposition to the notion of original sin was not an innovative contribution of the Enlightenment. Alan Jacobs aptly comments in his cultural history of the idea that no other doctrine, "not even the belief that some people are eternally damned," had generated as much hostility as original sin (*Original Sin: A Cultural History* [New York: HarperOne, 2008], xi).

project as a whole by saying that he rebuilt Christian dogmatics as an exercise in human psychology, with the notion of God-consciousness as its guiding principle.

The major text for understanding Schleiermacher on original sin is *The Christian Faith* (1830–31).[3] Central to Schleiermacher's understanding of sin is his understanding of human psychology. For Schleiermacher, human self-consciousness can be divided in two: the higher self-consciousness and the sensible self-consciousness. The latter is the human perception of the world and what we might call "feelings," or social and moral attitudes to the world around us;[4] the former is the site of Schleiermacher's famous "feeling of absolute dependence" or "God consciousness," which is the awareness that our freedom and spontaneity come from a source outside ourselves.[5] It is important to note that this higher consciousness never actually exists in the abstract, but always exists in connection to the sensible self-consciousness. This is important, because it is in the relationship between these two that Schleiermacher locates the problem of sin.

He defines sin as follows:

> The evil condition can only consist in an obstruction or arrest of the vitality of the higher self-consciousness, so that there comes to be little or no union of it with the various determinations of the sensible self-consciousness, and thus little or no religious life. We may give to this condition, in its most extreme form, the name of *Godlessness*, or, better, *God-forgetfulness*.[6]

3. *The Christian Faith*, trans. H. R. Mackintosh and J. S. Stewart (Edinburgh: T&T Clark, 1989), hereafter *CF*, with references to chapter and paragraph.
4. *CF* 5.1.
5. *CF* 4.3.
6. *CF* 11.2.

In other words, Schleiermacher is saying that it is possible for the sensible self-consciousness to become so preoccupied with the things of this world, the relationships that exist between the human subject and its various objects, that the God-consciousness can simply drop from view entirely. Men and women can be so immersed in their own lives, their own joys, sorrows, desires, and frustrations, that they lose all sense of their dependence on something greater than themselves for their freedom.

Given this, we might characterize Schleiermacher's view of sin as being something that essentially stunts the growth to psychological maturity of humans. This connects to his Christology, in which Christ is the supreme example of perfect God-consciousness and therefore the basis on which Schleiermacher can defend the superiority of Christianity over other monotheistic religions. It also decisively shapes his understanding of original sin.

When he discusses Adam and Eve, Schleiermacher demonstrates an indifference to whether they were historical figures or not. In part, this is because of the rather narrow task he assigns to dogmatics, which is not to make a judgment on the interpretation of Scripture as such.[7] Yet this is not Schleiermacher's only criticism of the received confessional tradition. He sees the traditional teaching as itself incoherent. First, Adam's "sinful nature" must have preceded the first sin because of the ease with which the first pair fell. Indeed, he sees this as a problem that intensifies as one takes the narrative more literally, on the grounds that he regards the temptation as trivial and easy to avoid.[8] Second, he regards as nonsensical the notion that something was fundamentally changed in human nature by the sin of the first

7. "As regards the Mosaic narrative: in accordance with the limits which we have assigned to Dogmatics, that science cannot be expected to determine how the said record is to be interpreted and whether it purports to be history or allegory" (*CF* 72.5).
8. *CF* 72.2.

187

man: individuals can only act in accordance with their nature; if the individual appears to change the nature of a species, then either the initial definition of the species was inadequate or the individual has been wrongly classified as belonging to that species.[9] Schleiermacher allows the logical possibility that the change in human nature could have been wrought by an external agent—that is, the Devil—but this he sees as plunging Christian theology into Manichaeism.[10]

If original sin is not to be understood as involving the decisive primeval act of a historical Adam that fundamentally altered human nature, then how is it to be understood? Schleiermacher sees the story of Adam and Eve as paradigmatic for subsequent generations: Eve represents the ease with which the sensuous dimension of human psychology is easily led to oppose the God-consciousness by external temptations. Adam represents how easily sin is assimilated by imitation even without great external pressure, but simply through a forgetfulness of God.[11]

Schleiermacher's denial that human nature is fundamentally changed by the fall raises the obvious question of how sin can come to be known as sin. In earlier, orthodox theology, the pre-fall Adam had functioned as a kind of benchmark against which the post-fall human race could be measured: rather than being devoted to God and obedient to his commands, Adam (and thus his posterity) had chosen to rebel, a rebellion epitomized by the first act of disobedience in eating the forbidden fruit. For Schleiermacher, however, humanity has always shared the same basic nature, and the account of the fall serves merely as a paradigm of the individual fall of every human.[12] What this does, of course, is

9. *CF* 72.3.
10. *CF* 72.3.
11. *CF* 72.5.
12. *CF* 72.5.

to push the theologian to look not to Adam as the benchmark for judging sin but rather to Christ, who, as the supreme example of the perfect God-consciousness, becomes himself the standard by which sin can then be judged. Even if we allow that the first man had not committed an actual sin, yet the psychological preparation behind each act of sin would be enough to prevent him being a kind of benchmark for human perfection.[13] Only because the God-consciousness has been fully and perfectly revealed in Christ can we know what the depth of human imperfection is.[14]

Schleiermacher's understanding of sin is complex, but its significance can be summarized very briefly. Sin is a disruption of human psychology, not primarily an offense against God; there was no golden age prior to Adam's fall (and, indeed, the historicity of Adam is itself a matter of dogmatic indifference) and thus humans were created as fallen; Adam is a paradigm of what it is to be a human, and Christ becomes the great paradigm of what it is to be a human with perfect God-consciousness, a model of that to which all should aspire. There is thus an impulse within the type of theology set forth by Schleiermacher to see the essence or outworking of Christian salvation as one defined above all by practical ethics.

Walter Rauschenbusch (1861–1918)

In the English-speaking world, Schleiermacher's understanding of original sin and its consequences received its most influential expression in the work of Walter Rauschenbusch (1861–1918). Wrestling with the social problems created by various nineteenth-century developments—urbanization, industrialization, militarism, and so on—Rauschenbusch sought to recast

13. *CF* 94.1.
14. *CF* 94.2.

Christian doctrine in a manner that would make it a dynamic force for social change. In so doing, he became the primary advocate of what has become known as the social gospel. He articulates his view of sin most clearly and concisely in *A Theology for the Social Gospel*, which he originally delivered as the Taylor Lectures at Yale in 1917.[15]

Central to Rauschenbusch's theology is the concept of the kingdom of God. This makes it clear from the outset that his concern is not with individual salvation (and thus, by inference, with individual sin), but rather with the corporate notion of society. The teaching of Christ was focused on the advent of the kingdom, on the transformation of society as a whole, based on an ethic of love.[16] In taking this view, Rauschenbusch stands in the line stemming from Schleiermacher as refracted through Albrecht Ritschl.[17]

When he approaches the subject of sin, Rauschenbusch operates with the basic psychological categories that he has inherited from Schleiermacher. Ironically, from a later perspective, this allows him to criticize those social gospel advocates who try to reduce sin to a function of environment: Rauschenbusch sees this attempt as analogous to the traditional view of original sin, in its passing final

15. The lectures have been reprinted as *A Theology for the Social Gospel* (Louisville: Westminster John Knox, 1997), hereafter *TSG*.

16. Commenting on traditional "individualistic" theology, he declares, "What a spectacle, that the original teaching of our Lord has become an incongruous element in so-called evangelical theology, like a stranger with whom the other doctrines would not associate" (*TSG*, 25). In this context, he singles out Britain, which had dominated world capitalism for over a century, as having an individualistic theology that served to undergird the established order rather than to critique it (*TSG*, 29).

17. In the generation after Schleiermacher, the most significant theologian was undoubtedly Albrecht Ritschl (1822–89). Ritschl developed Schleiermacher's insights into sin and salvation and placed the kingdom of God, as anticipated in the practical ethics of Christ, as the key to Christianity; see N. P. Williams, *The Ideas of the Fall and Original Sin* (London: Longmans, Green and Co., 1927), 438–39. On Ritschl's view of sin, see Donald L. Mueller, *An Introduction to the Theology of Albrecht Ritschl* (Philadelphia: Westminster, 1969), 63–77.

responsibility for sin to something outside the individual.[18] Nevertheless, he is also concerned that an overemphasis on individual sin, manifest in the individual consciousness of sin, has led to a trivialization of what it is that sin consists of and thus what righteousness consists of. Thus, he says, one minister identifies good works with church attendance, Bible reading, and financial support for public worship; another defines sin as drinking, gambling, and going to the theater; both miss the larger abuses perpetrated by the capitalist system in their home city of New York. In short, Rauschenbusch is interested in exposing structural, institutional sin.[19]

In his analysis of sin, Rauschenbusch is convinced that the significance of the fall of Adam has been massively overstated in later theology. We noted above that Schleiermacher regarded the question of Adam's historicity as of no systematic importance whatsoever. In *A Theology for the Social Gospel*, Rauschenbusch does not explicitly deny the historicity of Adam, but that would seem to be the obvious inference of his statement that the story of the fall originated in the ninth century BC as an attempt to provide a rationale for the origins not of sin but of death and evil. He also points to the fact that the fall fulfills little structural role within the theology of the Old Testament. Thus, he combines both text criticism and post-Gablerian biblical theology in his assault on the traditional doctrine of original sin.[20]

---

18. *TSG*, 33. Nevertheless, as one recent biographer has commented, "Rauschenbusch showed no interest in confronting the possibilities that the nature of humanity was corrupted in the sense spoken of by Paul and Augustine. He believed rather that evil manifested itself 'organically,' and in biological fashion was transmitted from one group to another. Once these social evils manifested themselves collectively within society, they were nearly impossible to overcome" (Christopher H. Evans, *The Kingdom Is Always but Coming: A Life of Walter Rauschenbusch* [Grand Rapids: Eerdmans, 2004], 301–2).

19. *TSG*, 36.

20. *TSG*, 39–42. Johann Philipp Gabler (1753–1826) was a German biblical scholar often regarded as the founder of modern biblical theology. He made a clear

Two further things of interest emerge out of Rauschenbusch's discussion of the fall. First, it is clear that his notion of truth is, at root, profoundly pragmatic: he is not interested in what he would (no doubt) regard as speculative abstraction that makes no practical difference. The social gospel is above all things practical.

In other words, discussion of the fall as a historical event with decisive impact on all future generations is ultimately unnecessary; sin is a fact and Christians should concentrate on combating it rather than trying to explain it. There is more than a whiff of Marxist prioritizing of action over theory at this point.

Second, Rauschenbusch regards the traditional doctrine of the fall as inappropriately relativizing the sins of later generations, such as syphilis, government corruption, and imperialist wars. In this context, a fixation on a fall into sin at the start of history has actually blocked the ability of human beings to understand properly their own role, and the role of their own generation, in the perpetuation, development, and exacerbation of sin within society. In other words, the doctrine of original sin is not simply unbiblical; one might go so far as to declare it positively anti-Christian.[21]

Interestingly enough, he does believe in human solidarity: one of the things that should make each generation more self-critical and careful to combat its own sinful impulses is the legacy that will be left for future generations. Indeed, the ability of humans to combat sin effectively places great responsibility on their shoulders.[22]

When Rauschenbusch comes to define sin, the influence of Schleiermacher is clear: sin is selfishness, defined as the domi-

distinction between dogmatic theology and biblical theology, seeing the latter as the investigation of the beliefs expressed by individual authors and books in the Bible in their historical context.

21. *TSG*, 43.
22. *TSG*, 43.

nance of the sensual nature over the higher, spiritual nature.[23] He is more emphatic than Schleiermacher in drawing out the social implications of this point: sin, in its most developed forms, is a conflict between the individual ego and the common good of humanity.[24] This in turn leads him to make explicit his understanding of God: God is the common good of humanity. There is no "God out there" for Rauschenbusch, at least not in any sense that is meaningful or relevant for humans and thus for their theology. God is to be identified with society as it is properly ordered in terms of its common good. The heir of Hegel and German idealism, Rauschenbusch effectively identifies God with the goal of human history.[25] In this context, he predictably demonstrates a flexible and historicist approach to the Decalogue: the first table (telling of humans' duty to God) is reduced to three commandments, because Christ declared the Sabbath an ordinance made for humans; polytheism and idol worship are no longer dangers; the misuse of God's name is of little account, now that sorcery is not widespread; and so the major thrust of biblical ethics is on the application of the second table—and these commands are all of social significance.[26]

This, of course, points to the fact that Rauschenbusch (like Schleiermacher and, even more so, Ritschl) regards sin as revealed not by the primeval fall of Adam but by a comparison of the world as it is with the ideal kingdom of God, which is to come and which was proleptically revealed in the life and teaching of

23. *TSG*, 45–46.
24. *TSG*, 47.
25. *TSG*, 49. "God is not only the spiritual representative of humanity; he is identified with it. . . . He works through humanity to realize his purposes, and our sins block and destroy the Reign of God in which he might fully reveal and realize himself. Therefore our sins against the least of our fellow-men in the last resort concern God."
26. *TSG*, 48–49.

the Lord Jesus Christ. Adam is for Rauschenbusch too shad-
owy a figure, and the details of his prelapsarian life and virtues
are too brief, for him to provide a sound measure by which to
understand sin and its impact. By contrast, the kingdom provides
just such a measure.[27]

The kingdom is marked by two characteristics: love and the
commonwealth of labor.[28] In fact, of course, these two characteristics are functionally one and the same: love considered in
isolation is an abstract concept that has no real, positive content.
For Rauschenbusch, love is the establishment and propagation
of appropriate labor relations. In other words, the kingdom (and
therefore God himself) looks rather like a late nineteenth-century
vision of a socialist utopia, and sin looks rather like the selfish
acquisition of property and capital, which should really be shared
magnanimously among everyone.[29] The vertical dimension of
sin as an offense against a holy God is entirely subsumed under
the horizontal aspect of sin as dysfunctional social relationships
with fellow humans.

Given all of this, one might have expected Rauschenbusch
to have reduced the idea of the transmission of sin down to a
matter of imitation. Certainly, he wishes to avoid any hint of
shifting responsibility away from the individual agent and onto
the action of some primeval ancestor in the garden of Eden. Yet
he also wants to avoid a simplistic Pelagianism that does not take
seriously the pervasive nature of sin. Thus, he emphasizes the
powerful and determinative impact on the individual of social
relations that cultivate and reinforce sinful behavior. Indeed,
he can even use the biological metaphor for talking about the
transmission of sin, but he does so in a very distinctive way, as

27. *TSG*, 51.
28. *TSG*, 54.
29. *TSG*, 55.

merely an analogy with the way social structures and practices impact and mold the individual, apparently in a manner that is irresistible.[30]

Rauschenbusch's theology has had a profound and long-lasting impact on subsequent theology. Indeed, with his emphasis on what we might call structural or institutional sin, he is very much the precursor of modern theological concerns—liberal and indeed evangelical—with social justice and concepts such as institutional racism and sexism. His thought represents a popular and accessible outworking of Schleiermacher's essentially psychological understanding of the nature of sin and makes explicit the dogmatic implications of this: sin is not really a vertical problem but rather a horizontal one, a problem of not realizing one's full humanity here on earth. The note of it being a direct offense against a holy God is entirely missing. Sin is a direct offense against other humans and only indirectly, therefore, against God.

Karl Barth (1886–1968)

Karl Barth is without doubt the most significant Protestant dogmatician of the twentieth century, whose work has enjoyed something of a renaissance in the past twenty years, with the advent of postmodern and narrative theologies, as well as the interest in theological interpretation. His rebellion against the

---

30. "The permanent vices and crimes of adults are not transmitted by heredity, but by being socialized; for instance, alcoholism and all drug evils; cruel sports, such as bull-fights and pugilism; various forms of sex perversity; voluntary deformities, such as foot-binding, corseting, piercing of ears and nose; blood-feuds in Corsica; lynching in America. Just as syphilitic corruption is forced on the helpless foetus in its mother's womb, so these hereditary social evils are forced on the individual embedded in the womb of society and drawing his ideas, moral standards, and spiritual ideals from the general life of the social body" (*TSG*, 60).

kind of theology represented by Schleiermacher and Ritschl is well known. Yet, for all this rebellion, his thinking on sin retains certain continuities with the old liberalism.

In addressing the matter of original sin in his *Church Dogmatics*, Barth is happy to use the classical orthodox terminology.[31] Nevertheless, he is opposed to any idea that this might involve a kind of hereditary or biological defect and indeed commends later Reformed orthodoxy for arguing that the transmission of original sin is by imputation.[32] Despite this, however, Barth's construction of original sin is markedly different from that of classical Reformed orthodoxy in a number of ways.

First, there is the question of the actual historicity of Adam. Historicity in general in Barth's theology is a complicated matter. The reader of Barth is faced not only with the typical problems involved in reading a theologian whose corpus is vast and whose thought is often expressed in elliptical fashion; there is also the added complication of his famous distinction between *Historie* and *Geschichte* (loosely translated "saga"), which often gives his discussion of biblical narrative a somewhat slippery quality. This applies particularly to the biblical narrative of Eden, which Barth himself categorizes as *saga*. It is worth quoting his comments on this in full:

> Who could see and attest the coming into being of heaven and earth and especially the coming into being of Adam and his corresponding individual existence? It is not history but only

---

31. "There can be no objection to the Latin expression *peccatum originale* if it is not given this more exact definition. It is indeed quite adequate, telling us that we are dealing with the original and radical and therefore the comprehensive and total act of man, with the imprisonment of his existence in that circle of evil being and evil activity. In this imprisonment God speaks to him and makes Himself his liberator in Jesus Christ" (Karl Barth, *Church Dogmatics*, vol. 4, *The Doctrine of Reconciliation*, part 1, trans. G. W. Bromiley and T. F. Torrance [New York: T&T Clark, 1956], 500).

32. Ibid., 511.

saga which can tell us that he came into being in this way and existed as the one who came into being in this way—the first man. We miss the unprecedented and incomparable thing which the Genesis passages tell us of the coming into being and existence of Adam if we try to read and understand it as history, relating it either favourably or unfavourably to scientific palæontology, or to what we now know with some historical certainty concerning the oldest and most primitive forms of human life. The saga as a form of historical narration is a *genre* apart. And within this *genre* biblical saga is a special instance which cannot be compared with others but has to be seen and understood in and for itself. Saga in general is the form which, using intuition and imagination, has to take up historical narration at the point where events are no longer susceptible as such of historical proof.[33]

It would appear from this that Barth is using the concept of saga, rather than straightforward history, to bring out the fact that creation and the events and actions surrounding it have a significance beyond the mere narrative, that there is something unique, not analogous to anything else, that is going on here. This might, of course, mean that Barth does regard Adam as a historical figure but simply sees his uniqueness as overriding normal categories of history. That, however, is an unlikely reading.

First, Barth sees part of the key to understanding Adam to be an acceptance of the implications of the documentary hypothesis of the Pentateuch, which for him makes it clear that the events recounted should not be taken at face value.[34] Second, Barth

33. Ibid., 508.
34. "In the strict exegetical sense we ought not perhaps to combine the Yahwistic text of Gen. 3 with the passage Gen. 2:2–3 which belongs to the Priestly text. Otherwise we might observe that the seventh day of creation, the first day in the life of man, in which he had nothing to do but to keep the sabbath with God Himself in peace and joy and freedom, was followed at once by the day of his pride

explicitly rejects any notion that there was ever a point in time when creation was unfallen.[35] These two points, more than the language of saga, indicate his basic rejection of the historicity of the events and actions recounted in Genesis 1–3.

If Adam's significance is not tied to his historicity or to any actual moment in time when creation was indeed unfallen, what is the significance of Adam for Barth? In brief, Adam is everyman: in him we see ourselves; in his sin, we see our sin, our dilemma, our status outside of Christ. "Adam is not a fate which God has suspended over us. Adam is the truth concerning us as it is known to God and told to us."[36]

This points toward Barth's understanding of Adam as the representative human as expounded by Paul in Romans 5. Here, Barth's emphasis on Christ as the revelation of God causes him to reverse the standard ordering of Adam-Christ, where Christ comes as the one who fulfills that which Adam was appointed to do, but which he failed to do. In *Church Dogmatics*, Barth states that we should not talk of an Adam-Christ, but a Christ-Adam, parallel. Christ, he declares, is the original, Adam merely the figure of him who was to come.[37]

This parallel receives a much fuller exposition in a separate work of Barth, *Christ and Adam*.[38] Here Barth makes it clear

---

and fall as the first day of his own will and work and activity and achievement. It is, however, not merely legitimate but necessary to combine Gen. 3 with Gen. 2:5–25, and therefore to say that man had hardly been formed of the dust of the earth and become a living soul by the breath of God, that he had hardly been put in the garden of Eden and charged to dress it and to keep it, that his creation had hardly been completed by that of the woman as an indispensable and suitable helpmeet, before he followed up and directly opposed all the good things that God had done for him by becoming disobedient to God" (ibid., 508–9).

35. Ibid., 508.

36. Ibid., 511.

37. Ibid., 512–13.

38. Karl Barth, *Christ and Adam: Man and Humanity in Romans 5*, trans. T. A. Smail (New York: Collier, 1962).

that Adam is in no sense a revelation of true human nature, which then goes bad and requires rescuing via Christ. Rather, Adam is the revelation of what we are outside of Christ, who is himself the archetypal man, the true and foundational revelation of humanity.[39]

This position has numerous systematic implications. First, by prioritizing Christ over Adam in Romans 5 in this way, Barth seems to be pushing in a universalist direction, as the relation of Christ to humanity must surely be as inclusive as that of Adam to humanity, even if Barth does not care to draw out explicitly what might appear to others to be the obvious soteriological conclusion.[40]

Second, this once again undercuts any need for Adam to be a historical figure or for the fall to be a historical event in the conventional sense of the term. There is no moment of "fall" within time. We are in a very real sense not simply *in* Adam, but are actually Adam, in that all of our lives are simply repetitions of his: "We are what Adam was and so are all our fellow men. And the one Adam is what we and all men are. Man is at once an individual and only an individual, and, at the same time, without in any way losing his individuality, he is the responsible representative of all men."[41]

Though Barth professedly breaks with the tradition of theology that stems from Schleiermacher, there are still points of affinity that exist between the two. The irrelevance of the historicity of Adam, the rejection of the idea that man was ever unfallen, the concern for avoiding any notion of biological heredity relative to sin, and the assumption that nothing must imply that humans

39. Ibid., 39–41.
40. This is the argument of John Murray in his review of *Christ and Adam*. See *The Collected Writings of John Murray*, vol. 4 (Edinburgh: Banner of Truth, 1982), 319 (a part of an overall argument that spans pages 316–21).
41. Barth, *Christ and Adam*, 113; see also 40.

are in any way to be held to account for alien guilt are all clear in Barth's treatment of the topic. It also seems at least arguable that Barth's view of sin retains sin's fundamental character as an attitude of mind—a psychological or existential category.

Rudolf Bultmann (1884–1976)

Rudolf Bultmann was arguably the most influential New Testament scholar/theologian of the twentieth century. His understanding of original sin is shaped both by his distinctive understanding of the intellectual roots of aspects of New Testament thought and by his appropriation of certain aspects of existentialist philosophy.

For example, in dealing with the notion of a historical fall of a pristine, innocent creation, Bultmann ascribes such a narrative concept to the influence of Gnosticism on the formation of the New Testament.[42] The historicity of the fall is thus of no real significance to the theological lessons that Bultmann seeks to draw from the biblical account. In fact, the fall is part of the "mythical world picture" presented by the Bible that no longer fulfills a useful explanatory purpose in the modern day.[43] Further, he has no hesitation in saying that Paul's account of original sin is itself incoherent. On the one hand, Paul simply assumes the reality that all are indeed sinners, without positing any cause for this. On the other, he locates the cause in the sin of Adam. Here, Bultmann argues, Paul is in thrall to Gnostic

42. Rudolf Bultmann, *Theology of the New Testament*, vol. 1, trans. Kendrick Grobel (New York: Scribner's, 1951), 172–73.

43. Rudolf Bultmann, "New Testament Mythology: The Problem of Demythologizing the New Testament Proclamation," in *New Testament Mythology and Other Basic Writings*, trans. Schubert Ogden (Philadelphia: Fortress, 1984), 1–43.

mythology, although Bultmann credits Paul with avoiding positing something behind the sin of Adam that might reinforce a Gnostic theology.[44] The reason for this is that in Romans 5 Paul is trying to explain the universality not of sin but of death, and because he has argued that death is the punishment for Adam's sin, he is thus required to explain the universality of sin. This is further complicated by the fact that Paul also wants to make death the consequence of individual sin.[45] In this context, Bultmann understands sin as the condition of human existence whereby individuals seek to find fulfillment in themselves and for themselves.[46]

As with Schleiermacher, Bultmann sees no transmission of sin in the traditional, Augustinian sense: sin is and always has been the condition of humanity. Behind this lies the typical modern concern for the idea of one person being considered guilty because of the failure of another.[47] Much more explicitly than Schleiermacher, however, Bultmann dismisses the historicity of the fall: it is a mythical story, a means whereby an early era was able to make sense of the universality not so much of sin as of death.

Reinhold Niebuhr (1892–1971)

Reinhold Niebuhr wrote extensively about the nature of sin, something that contributed to his image as that of a theological

44. Bultmann, *Theology of the New Testament*, 250–51. In making this comment, Bultmann surely makes an implicit contrast between Paul's account of the fall and that given in Gen. 3, where the agency of the serpent is clearly important (thus making the narrative presumably more "Gnostic" on Bultmann's terms!).

45. Ibid., 252.

46. Ibid., 246–48, 253.

47. "At the most, men sinning under the curse of Adam's sin could be regarded as guilty only in a legal sense, inasmuch as law deals only with the guilty deed; but then we would have no right to speak of guilt in the ethical sense" (ibid., 251).

pessimist. His most famous discussion of original sin occurs in volume 1 of *The Nature and Destiny of Man: A Christian Interpretation*, which began as the Gifford Lectures for 1939.[48]

Niebuhr's discussion of sin draws heavily on Kierkegaard's *The Concept of Anxiety*. At the heart of the Christian doctrine lies the dilemma of inevitability and freedom: Christianity wishes to maintain both in order to underline the tragic condition of fallen humans and yet the responsibility of individuals for their sin.[49] For Niebuhr, following Kierkegaard, sinfulness is the result of the fact that humans are conscious, reflective beings who have the capacity to transcend the natural processes in which they are involved; thus they are constantly tempted to despair. In what Niebuhr calls a *quantitative* development of life, humans seek to escape their finiteness and weakness. We might characterize this as seeking to transcend their existence through finite, earthly means—for example, materialism, entertainment, power, sex, and money. In fact, humans transcend themselves only through a *qualitative* development of life in their submission to the will of God.[50] Quantitative development is the sin of self-love, and the sin of self-love presupposes a prior lack of trust in God.[51]

Niebuhr does reference the sin of Adam in this context: "The sin of each individual is preceded by the sin of Adam," he comments, but then completes the sentence with "but even this first sin of history is not the first sin."[52] In short, sin is paradoxically there in nature from the very beginning; there is no "fall" in history that would introduce evil into creation.

48. Reinhold Niebuhr, *The Nature and Destiny of Man: A Christian Interpretation*, 2 vols. (Louisville: Westminster John Knox, 1996).
49. Ibid., 1:243.
50. Ibid., 1:251.
51. Ibid., 1:252.
52. Ibid., 1:254.

Niebuhr makes this explicit in his subsequent discussion of what he characterizes as "literalistic errors." While Niebuhr has no time for the moralism of Pelagian theology, which does not take seriously the tragic inevitability of sin, he regards the Augustinian notion of original sin, as something inherited, to be hopelessly tied to an understanding of the fall as literally historical and as fundamentally altering human nature. Niebuhr does appreciate the Augustinian motivation in this: the rejection of any ground for human pride.[53] Yet Niebuhr still regards commitment to historicity as wrong. Instead, he sets the notion of Adam as representative man in opposition to that of Adam as historical man. By this, he is not implying that Adam plays the role of a federal representative, as in the covenant theology of the seventeenth century—that would assume Adam's historical reality. Rather, he sees Adam as the archetypal representative of the way in which all humans sin. In this, it is true that his concern is not primarily with the historical difficulties of maintaining Adam's historicity, but rather with the destruction of freedom that the notion of inherited sin would seem to bring with it.[54] Nevertheless, he does explicitly reject any notion that Adam was a historical figure and that the fall was a historical event.[55]

Niebuhr regards commitment to a historical fall as analogous to pagan myths about a golden age, which can then function as the criterion for judging the defection of all future epochs. Indeed, he even sees it as connecting to the nostalgic psychology of adulthood, which looks back to a mythic, idyllic childhood as providing individuals with knowledge of their true, authentic

53. Ibid., 1:279.
54. Ibid., 1:26–64.
55. "Christian theology has found it difficult to refute the rationalistic rejection of the myth of the Fall without falling into the literalistic error of insisting upon the Fall as an historical event" (ibid., 1:267–68).

natures.[56] Like Schleiermacher, he finds the idea of the fall, as fundamentally changing human nature, to be something that is incoherent: Catholicism attempts to avoid this by stressing the fall as the loss of a superadded gift of grace, Protestantism as the loss of the image of God. Neither position does justice to the fact that sin is the corruption of humanity's true essence, but not its destruction. Instead, Niebuhr points to the fall as having not chronological but vertical significance.[57] By implication, Adam is thus the paradigm, the great example of the choice that lies before all humans and of the wrong decision made in the face of that choice.[58]

If Adam provides no example of humanity in a pre-fall state, the question for Niebuhr becomes where such an example of perfected humanity can be found. Where are we to look for the criterion of what it is to be a perfect human? The answer, of course, is Christ. As in the view of Schleiermacher and his successors, it is Jesus Christ who really represents humanity as it should be. This has a threefold aspect. First, Christ provides the standard by which we know the true possibilities of life and, indeed, therefore the lost perfections of Adam.[59] Second, Christ on the cross represents the intrusion of selfless love into history, something that stands in judgment on attempts to transcend the self from within the framework of nature, and an exposé of the gap between human self-assertion and divine love.[60] Finally, it points to the fact that the kingdom will be fulfilled in history, not in some form of otherworldly mysticism.[61] For Niebuhr, this

56. Ibid., 1:268.
57. Ibid., 1:268–69.
58. See ibid., 1:278: "Perfection before the Fall is, in other words, perfection before the act."
59. Ibid., 2:76–77.
60. Ibid., 2:81–90.
61. Ibid., 2:90–95.

means social and political activism; though, with his emphasis on individual sin as a form of Kierkegaardian anxiety, this is clearly not set on quite the optimistic anthropological footing that we noted in Rauschenbusch.

Wolfhart Pannenberg (1928–2014)

In comparison to that of Barth and Bultmann, the theology of Wolfhart Pannenberg marks something of a return to the classic liberal concerns of Schleiermacher and Ritschl, particularly with regard to the importance of historical-critical issues.

His major treatment of original sin is in the second volume of his *Systematic Theology*.[62] For Pannenberg, the story of Adam is not a story about the origin of sin in the sense that it offers an explanation of the universality of human guilt and corruption based on the sin of one man and understood in Augustinian or federal terms. Indeed, as for Scheiermacher, the historicity of Adam seems to be for Pannenberg an issue of dogmatic indifference; his theology has no need for it. Rather, Adam stands as the great paradigm of the psychology of sinful action: Adam was deceived into thinking that he could find his fulfillment in his own finite resources, and that is the deception that reflects the psychology of all of us.[63] In this sense, Pannenberg is the heir

---

62. Wolfhart Pannenberg, *Systematic Theology*, trans. Geoffrey W. Bromiley, 3 vols. (Grand Rapids: Eerdmans, 1994).

63. "We engage in sin because of the deception. Our voluntary committing of it is enough to make us guilty. There does not have to be a primal and once-for-all event of a fall for which Adam was guilty quite apart from all entanglement in sin. . . . In this sense the story of Adam is the story of the whole race. It is repeated in each individual. The point is not Adam's first state of innocence in contrast to that of his descendants" (Pannenberg, *Systematic Theology*, 2:263). See Stanley J. Grenz, *Reason for Hope: The Systematic Theology of Wolfhart Pannenberg* (Oxford: Oxford

of Schleiermacher and the nineteenth-century liberal tradition stemming therefrom.

Pannenberg sees the connection between Adam and individual humans as one of participation by emulation: we participate in Adam's sin by sinning in the same way as he did. The obvious christological implication is that humans are united to Christ by being changed into his likeness.[64] With a greater sensitivity to historical process and eschatology, Pannenberg is critical of Schleiermacher for not really giving significance to the historical actions of Christ, particularly the distinction between his pre- and postresurrection significance, and for focusing rather exclusively on Jesus' God-consciousness.[65] Pannenberg's own solution is, however, not so much a rejection of the paradigmatic nature of Christ's God-consciousness as an enriching of it: the death of Christ is a revelation to others that they no longer have to see themselves as excluded from fellowship with God. Through accepting their own finitude as Jesus did, and in fellowship with him, they now share in eternal life with the assurance that death will be overcome. Pannenberg's theology is Schleiermacher with a Hegelian/historical eschatological twist.[66]

Some Concluding Thoughts

As noted at the beginning of this essay, modern theology is a highly diverse phenomenon, and I make no claim that the theologians treated above offer a comprehensive view of mod-

University Press, 1990), 104–6; also E. Frank Tupper, *The Theology of Wolfhart Pannenberg* (Philadelphia: Westminster, 1973), 72–74.

64. Pannenberg, *Systematic Theology*, 2:304.
65. Ibid., 2:308.
66. Ibid., 2:434. See the discussion of sin as connecting to Christology and eschatology in Tupper, *Theology of Pannenberg*, 161–62, 182–83.

ern positions on original sin. Nevertheless, the examples given are instructive because they do highlight certain axioms and emphases that pervade modern theological discussions.

All of the theologians discussed stand in continuity with certain aspects of Enlightenment critiques of classical orthodoxy. First, all of them repudiate any notion that humanity stands guilty before God because of the imputation of an alien guilt—the guilt of a historical man called Adam to all of his descendants. By the standards of Enlightenment thought, such an imputation would be unethical. Even Barth, while seeing the language of imputation as an improvement on notions of inherited sin, sees this imputation not as built on the actions of a historical person, but rather as reflecting the archetypal, paradigmatic nature of Adam's sin.

Second, all of the theologians reject the relevance of the historicity of Adam. Whether this is because it is considered of no dogmatic importance, as in Schleiermacher, or because it is rejected outright, as in Bultmann and Pannenberg, is really of little account. All regard the idea of a creation that existed in a pristine state, prior to a historical action by a human agent that caused it to fall, as nonsense.

These two basic points serve to give modern treatments of original sin certain common features. First, there is no movement from innocence to guilt and condemnation in history. Creation was imperfect from the beginning. This has clear implications, not only for how one understands the first chapters of Genesis (and, indeed, the trajectory of the drama of Genesis beyond chapter 3), but also for one's understanding of the doctrine of God.

Second, human nature in and of itself is always fallen, and Adam functions therefore as a paradigm to which we all conform. This is not to say that modern theology is a species of Pelagianism. The emphasis on creation as always fallen and the repudiation of any notion of a pristine world before a historical fall mean that accusations of Pelagianism, with its commitment to the basic moral soundness of humanity, are not appropriate. Nevertheless, the repudiation of notions of alien guilt and the rejection of any notion that sin is transmitted by heredity or biology mean that Adam functions as the great example of the way in which we all sin and all fall.

Third, treatments of original sin give modern theology a christological focus. If there is no primeval world by which one is able to judge the depth of humanity's fall, then that role comes to be fulfilled by Christ. Whether he functions as the great paradigm of perfect God-consciousness or as the man-before-God of Barth, Christ comes to have priority in discussions of sin.

Fourth, modern theology attenuates the nature of sin. In these modern accounts, there is very little that points toward sin as being something done *against God*. In Schleiermacher, sin is a defective psychological state; in Rauschenbusch (and in modern political and feminist theologies), sin is something done by people against other people. Bultmann and Barth both employ the rhetoric about the seriousness of sin and the judgment of God, but it is hard to square this with their view that creation was itself defective and fallen. In traditional Christian orthodoxy, sin is an action that is a personal affront to a holy and righteous God, and it is that precisely because it involves a perversion of nature as he intended it to be and, indeed, as he created it to be.

Fifth, it is arguable that one of the perceived problems in orthodox dogmatics against which modern theology has reacted—the injustice of alien guilt—is not actually solved by these modern reconstructions. If there never was a time when humanity existed in a pristine state, then one wonders how these theologies are really an improvement on those that rooted the human dilemma in the sin of Adam imputed to or inherited by later generations. If it is unethical to hold me to account for the action of a primeval ancestor, then why is it morally preferable that I be held responsible for my sin if that is indeed simply the result of my status at birth, of me being merely a human creature?[67] What does it mean to say that I am responsible as an individual for my sinful state when it is actually a structural part of the original creation? And this, of course, has implications for how one understands redemption, implications that lie beyond the scope of this essay.[68] Contra Schleiermacher, the historicity of Adam is not a matter outside of the scope, or irrelevant to, the dogmatic task.[69]

In conclusion, one can perhaps summarize this survey by saying that modern theology witnesses to the fact, as clearly implied by Paul in Romans 5, that one's understanding of original sin is necessarily and decisively connected to the structure of one's theology as a whole. One's views of the historicity of Adam inevitably stand in positive connection to one's view of creation, to whether there was a fall in history or whether sin/alienation from God is part of the natural order. The nature and status of

67. See the comment of G. C. Berkouwer, aimed specifically at Schleiermacher and Ritschl, stating that, in attempts to explain the universality of the spread of sin on the basis of man's nature, the full gravity of sin is attenuated (*Sin*, trans. Philip C. Holtrop [Grand Rapids: Eerdmans, 1971], 525–26).

68. See J. P. Versteeg, "If Adam may no longer be viewed as a historical person but in him is revealed only what is inherent in every man, so that . . . one can hardly still talk about guilt in the proper sense of the word, then the character of redemption also naturally changes" (*Adam in the New Testament: Mere Teaching Model or First Historical Man*, 2nd ed., trans. Richard B. Gaffin Jr. [Phillipsburg, NJ: P&R, 2012], 65).

69. See the comment of J. van Genderen and W. H. Velema: "The abandonment of the historicity of Paradise and the fall of Adam and Eve into sin repeatedly proves to have far-reaching consequences for various aspects of the dogmatics" (*Concise Reformed Dogmatics*, trans. Gerrit Bilkes and Ed M. van der Maas [Phillipsburg, NJ: P&R, 2008], 388).

Adam are foundational to one's understanding of biblical theology. It is perhaps fitting to close with the words with which J. P. Versteeg ends his own important monograph on the theological importance of Adam to the biblical (and dogmatic) scheme:

> To be occupied with the question of how Scripture speaks about Adam is thus anything but an insignificant problem of detail. As the first historical man and head of humanity, Adam is not mentioned merely in passing in the New Testament. The redemptive-historical correlation between Adam and Christ determines the framework in which . . . the redemptive work of Christ has its place. That work of redemption can no longer be confessed according to the meaning of Scripture, if it is divorced from the framework in which it stands there. Whoever divorces the work of redemption from the framework in which it stands in Scripture no longer allows the Word to function as the norm that determines *everything*. There has been no temptation through the centuries to which theology has been more exposed than this temptation. There is no danger that theology has more to fear than this danger.[70]

70. Versteeg, *Adam in the New Testament*, 67.

ALLIANCE®
OF CONFESSING EVANGELICALS

What is the Alliance?

The Alliance of Confessing Evangelicals is a coalition of pastors, scholars, and churchmen who hold to the historic creeds and confessions of the Reformed faith and who proclaim biblical doctrine in order to foster a Reformed awakening in today's church. Our members join for gospel proclamation, biblically sound doctrine, fostering of reformation, and the glory of God. We work and serve the church through media, events, and publishing.

The work started in media: *The Bible Study Hour* with James Boice, *Every Last Word* featuring Philip Ryken, *Mortification of Spin* with Carl Trueman and Todd Pruitt, *No Falling Word* with Liam Goligher, and *Dr. Barnhouse & the Bible* with Donald Barnhouse. These broadcasts air throughout North America as well as online at AllianceNet.org.

PlaceforTruth.org is our online magazine—a free, "go-to" theological resource. ChristwardCollective.org is a theological conversation equipping believers for growth. And reformation21.org provides cultural and church criticism. Our online daily devotionals include *Think and Act Biblically* and *Making God's Word Plain*, as well as MatthewHenry.org, a resource fostering biblical prayer.

Our events include the Philadelphia Conference on Reformed Theology, the oldest continuing national Reformed conference in North America, and regional events including theology and Bible conferences. Pastors' events, such as reformation societies, continue to encourage, embolden, and equip church leaders in pursuit of reformation in the church.

Alliance publishing includes books from trustworthy authors, with titles such as *Zeal for Godliness*, *Our Creed*, and more. We offer a vast list of affordable booklets, as well as e-books such as *Learning to Think Biblically* and *How to Live a Holy Life*. And we encourage sound biblical doctrine by offering a wide variety of CD and MP3 resources.